From Seller to Leader

Navigating Your New Sales Management Role

Author: Ray Erens

First printing, December 2023.

ISBN: 978-0-7961-3525-4 (Paperback)

ISBN: 978-0-7961-3525-4 (eBook)

Positive Mindset

Personal Growth

Published by Positive Mindset Books

40 Lazuriet Crescent.

Ennerdale, Johannesburg, South Africa, 1830

www.positivemindsetbooks.com

Table of Contents

Introduction

Over my many years of sales leadership, I have seen many bright salespeople elevated to sales leadership roles because it is assumed that they will know what it takes for a sales team to be successful. Yes, many excelled in their new roles, but I have seen far too many fail miserably, not due to incompetence or a lack of understanding of sales but rather due to a lack of leadership abilities.

In my experience, I have observed that being a successful salesperson does not automatically translate into being an effective leader. Sales leadership requires a unique set of skills, such as the ability to motivate and inspire a team, make strategic decisions, and effectively communicate with different stakeholders. The purpose of this book is to provide practical guidance and insights on developing essential leadership abilities for individuals transitioning into sales management roles.

Welcome to Leadership

Congratulations on your promotion to the role of sales manager! As you step into this leadership position, you are embarking on a transformative journey that extends beyond the familiar territory of hitting individual sales targets. Welcome to a realm where the demands are as diverse as they are challenging, but so too is the excitement that comes with steering a team towards collective success.

In this role, you'll find yourself at the intersection of strategic planning and team dynamics, where your decisions shape not only your own success but that of your entire team.

The demands are manifold, from setting clear expectations and performance goals to navigating interpersonal dynamics and fostering a positive team culture. You'll be required to wear multiple hats, sometimes simultaneously acting as a mentor, coach, and strategist. Your ability to communicate effectively, both up and down the organisational hierarchy, becomes paramount, as does your skill in balancing authority with approachability.

The demands are not just confined to the professional arena; they extend into the realm of personal development. As a leader, you are not only responsible for the growth of your team but also for your own continuous learning. This dual commitment to personal and professional development is what makes leadership a dynamic and rewarding experience.

Amidst these demands, however, lies the excitement of shaping the future of your team and contributing to the overall success of the organisation. The thrill of seeing your team achieve and exceed targets, witnessing individual team members grow under your guidance, and knowing that your strategic decisions impact the company's trajectory—all of these elements contribute to the exhilaration of leadership.

Imagine the satisfaction of successfully navigating challenges, whether they be market fluctuations, changing customer expectations, or internal team dynamics. Each obstacle becomes an opportunity for growth, and your role as a leader is to guide your team through these challenges, emerging stronger and more cohesive on the other side.

Welcome to the dynamic world of leadership, where the demands are high, but so are the rewards. As you embark on this journey, "Elevate" is here to provide insights, strategies, and support to help you navigate the complexities and relish the excitement that comes with being at the helm of a successful sales team.

Understanding the Sales Manager Role

Before diving headlong into the challenges and triumphs of sales management, it's crucial to first grasp the essence of the role you're stepping into. As a sales manager, you're not just orchestrating the symphony of individual sales efforts; you're the conductor guiding the entire ensemble towards a harmonious crescendo of success. Your responsibilities extend far beyond closing deals; they encompass the strategic orchestration of your team's efforts, ensuring they align with overarching organisational goals.

Picture yourself as the linchpin between the frontline sales force and the executive leadership. Your role involves translating high-level organisational strategies into actionable plans for your team. It requires a nuanced understanding of market dynamics, customer needs, and the competitive landscape. You're no longer solely focused on your personal sales targets; your success is now measured by the collective achievements of your team.

Learning how to strike a balance between authoritative management and mentoring is essential for any sales manager. You're more than simply a boss; you're also your team's mentor and driving force. This requires a careful balancing act of doing things like guiding and supporting team members while also setting expectations and keeping them accountable. Your strategic expertise is essential, but so is your ability to create an environment where the team enjoys working together. It's about creating an environment where each team member may offer their individual abilities while working towards common objectives.

In essence, your role as a sales manager is akin to being the architect of success for your team. You design the framework for achievement, establish the parameters for individual and collective growth, and provide the support structure needed for your team to flourish. This means developing not only your own leadership skills but also understanding the strengths and weaknesses of each team member to leverage their full potential.

The sales manager role is dynamic, multifaceted, and central to the organisation's success. It demands a holistic perspective that extends beyond day-to-day operations. "Elevate" is here to guide you through this understanding, providing insights and strategies to navigate the complexities of your role with confidence and competence. As we delve deeper into the chapters ahead, remember that your success as a sales manager is intricately linked to your ability to comprehend, embrace, and excel in this multifaceted leadership role.

While sales leadership is complex and frequently mistaken for sales management, we'll go over the fundamental differences and how sales leaders are formed. In this book, I will attempt to cover all you need to know about sales leadership, including best practices, traits, habits, and key abilities that all sales leaders must possess in order to lead successful enterprise sales teams.

Any effective sales team must have strong sales leadership. A sales leader's responsibilities extend beyond simply overseeing a sales team. It entails offering leadership, direction, and support to guarantee that the team performs at its best while also encouraging each team member's professional progress. Sales leadership is critical since it can determine a company's ability to reach revenue targets and achieve long-term growth. Even the most competent sales team might struggle to accomplish its goals without good sales leadership.

Effective sales leadership entails far more than simply pushing your team to reach sales budgets. It entails gaining a thorough awareness of your team's strengths and shortcomings, forging strong bonds with team members, and establishing clear expectations and goals. Sales managers must also be skilled at fostering a positive team culture that promotes collaboration, open communication, and lifelong learning. The finest sales leaders motivate their teams to do their best by setting a good example, providing constructive comments, and recognising their team's achievements.

Although this seems like a huge challenge, you have been given this opportunity because others have faith in your abilities and have promoted or appointed you to this position. How you take advantage of this chance depends on how well you assess your current level of leadership abilities, particularly your interpersonal and emotional intelligence.

Chapter 1: Transitioning to Leadership

Navigating the Transition

There is no more challenging job change than moving from salesperson to sales manager. Overnight, the salesperson lost all autonomy and was replaced by a system in which his or her success was entirely dependent on the success of others. This is a stressful time for new sales managers. Senior leadership is asking you, "Where are your team's results?" And as you start to work along with your salespeople on a regular basis, it dawns on you that other salespeople don't approach the sales responsibility with the same level of skill and commitment as you did (Well, duh...this is why you got the promotion!)

Transitioning from a successful sales professional to a sales manager is a significant career shift, and it's not without its unique set of challenges. Understanding and effectively addressing these challenges is paramount for a smooth and successful transition.

One of the key challenges in transitioning to a leadership role is learning how to delegate tasks and trust your team members to carry out their responsibilities. This requires a shift in mindset from being solely responsible for your own work to overseeing and guiding the work of others. Additionally, developing strong communication skills is crucial in order to effectively convey expectations, provide feedback, and resolve conflicts within your team.

Let's examine a few of these challenges now.

Transitional Challenges: From Seller to Leader

1. Mindset Shift:

It is not uncommon for sales leaders to have risen to their position due to their own merits and qualities. However, when sales leaders are tasked with inspiring and motivating their people, fostering a focus on the long term, and facilitating change, they must adjust their perspective accordingly.

Adjusting to a new way of thinking is one of the key difficulties that must be overcome. When working in sales, it is common practice to place an emphasis on personal accomplishments, but when managing a team, one's success is dependent on the overall output of the group. An illustration of this would be making the mental shift from praising one's own sales successes to praising those of one's entire team. This can be a challenging adjustment.

2. Building Authority:

One of the distinct challenges faced by newly appointed sales managers is the delicate art of building authority within their team. As a sales professional, camaraderie with peers is often cultivated through shared successes and collaborative efforts. However, the transition to a managerial role necessitates a shift in power dynamics, and the need to establish authority without alienating former colleagues can be a nuanced process. This challenge extends beyond issuing directives; it involves inspiring respect, fostering a collaborative environment, and effectively leading the team towards collective success.

Establishing one's authority while avoiding alienating one's peers is a difficult balancing act. There is a possibility that some people on the team will question the established hierarchy that exists within the group. This is something that could happen. One approach to accomplishing this would be to provide constructive criticism to a colleague who was formerly your peer at work. However, this should be done in a manner that does not put a strain on the professional relationship that now exists between the two of you.

3. Balancing Responsibilities:

Finding the right balance between being hands-on with sales strategy and taking on the larger managerial responsibilities that come with the job is a major problem for newly promoted sales managers. Managerial responsibilities like performance reviews, strategic planning, and team development require time and focus, even if the excitement of closing deals still calls. Adjusting one's priorities and time management techniques may be necessary during this time of change. To help new sales managers properly combine their dual jobs and lead their teams to success, we delve into the challenges of achieving the correct balance in this chapter.

The difficulty lies in finding the optimal balance between being actively involved in the formulation of sales tactics and concentrating on managerial responsibilities such as conducting performance evaluations and fostering the growth of teams. As an example, consider balancing the time required to close agreements in order to meet targets with the time allotted for team coaching and strategy planning.

Strategies to tackle these challenges.

1. Invest in Leadership Training:

Strategy: Enrol in the programme that provides leadership training in order to obtain the necessary abilities. This could include holding workshops on topics such as effective communication, managing teams, and strategic thinking. Attending a seminar on leadership to gain the skills necessary to effectively motivate and direct a group of people is one example.

2. Open Communication:

Strategy: Make sure there is open communication among all members of the team. Make sure that your new responsibilities, expectations, and the direction you see the team going in are all communicated clearly.

Take, for instance, the practice of holding a team meeting to talk about the change, address any concerns, and establish ground rules for open and honest communication. This will create a safe and supportive environment where team members feel comfortable expressing their ideas, concerns, and feedback.

Additionally, encourage regular one-on-one check-ins with team members to foster open communication on an individual level and address any issues or challenges they may be facing.

3. Mentorship and Guidance:

Strategy: Seek the guidance of experienced sales managers both inside and outside of the company. It is likely to be of tremendous assistance to you to acquire the wisdom of those who have successfully navigated conditions that are comparable to those you are currently facing and come out on the other side. By establishing mentorship relationships, you can tap into a wealth of knowledge and gain valuable insights from those who have already overcome similar challenges. This guidance can provide you with practical approaches and advice to help navigate through any obstacles you may encounter in your new role.

Let's look at an example: Having regular meetings with a mentor in order to discuss challenges, receive advice, and gain new insights on how to be a successful leader is a great way to improve these skills. By establishing a strong mentor-mentee relationship, you can benefit from their experience and expertise, allowing you to learn from their successes and failures. Additionally, this ongoing support system can provide you with the encouragement and motivation needed to stay focused and determined in your pursuit of becoming a successful sales leader.

4. Delegate Effectively:

Learn the art of delegation. Identify tasks that can be assigned to team members, allowing you to focus on strategic aspects of your role. One important aspect of being a successful leader is the ability to delegate effectively. Delegating tasks and responsibilities to your team members not only helps you manage your workload more efficiently but also allows them to develop new skills and take on additional responsibilities.

By learning how to delegate effectively, you can empower your team members and foster a sense of ownership and accountability within the group. This can lead to increased productivity and a more cohesive team dynamic. Additionally, effective delegation can also help to identify potential future leaders within your team, as it allows individuals to showcase their abilities and take on more challenging tasks. By trusting your team members with important responsibilities, you are not only empowering them but also building their confidence and encouraging professional growth.

Take, for example, the practice of entrusting a member of the team with the responsibility of compiling routine sales reports so that the primary focus can be placed on developing long-term sales strategies.

5. Continuous Learning:

Adopt a mindset that is open to ongoing education as part of your strategy. Continue to educate yourself on the most recent developments in sales and leadership by keeping up with the latest books and webinars. This commitment to continuous learning will not only enhance your knowledge and skills but also demonstrate your dedication to personal and professional growth.

Additionally, seeking out mentorship or networking opportunities within the industry can provide valuable insights and guidance for further development in sales and leadership. Keeping up with the latest best practices can be achieved, for example, by subscribing to trade publications and developing a habit of reading management and leadership books.

6. Celebrate Team Success:

The strategy is to shift the focus from recognising individual accomplishments to celebrating the triumphs of the team. Develop a culture that places a high priority on working together and providing support to one another. By celebrating team success, it fosters a sense of camaraderie and encourages collaboration among team members. This not only boosts morale but also enhances overall productivity and creates a positive work environment.

Furthermore, it allows individuals to feel valued and appreciated for their contributions, which in turn increases employee satisfaction and loyalty. Consider, as an example of the practice, the tradition of publicly praising and recognising each team member's achievement upon the accomplishment of a common objective.

By recognising these challenges and implementing these strategies, a new sales manager can navigate the transition with greater confidence, fostering a positive and effective leadership style within the team. "Elevate" will delve further into these strategies, providing additional insights and practical advice to help you overcome the hurdles of this crucial career shift.

Building Credibility

Building credibility is essential for a new sales manager, as it establishes trust and fosters a positive working relationship with the sales team. This can be achieved by setting clear expectations, leading by example, and actively listening to the team's feedback and concerns. Additionally, maintaining credibility requires consistent communication, transparency, and delivering on promises to build trust over time.

Below are some key points that can help in a new sales leader's quest to build credibility:

- Building credibility is an essential aspect of a new sales manager's role. They must establish themselves as knowledgeable and trustworthy to gain the respect and confidence of their team members.

- One strategy for building credibility is through effective communication. Clear and transparent communication helps managers convey their expectations, goals, and vision, fostering trust among team members.

- Another way to build credibility is by demonstrating expertise in the field. A sales manager can enhance their knowledge through continuous learning and staying updated on industry trends.

- Building strong relationships with team members can also contribute to building credibility as a manager. By showing genuine interest in their well-being and actively supporting their professional growth, managers can earn the respect and confidence of their team.

- Acting ethically and displaying high moral standards is another important aspect of establishing credibility as a manager. Being consistent in making fair decisions, treating everyone equitably, and upholding ethical values fosters trust among team members.

- Taking responsibility for one's own actions is absolutely necessary in order to build credibility with the other members of the team.

Balancing authority with approachability

You should strive to be personable while still maintaining the authority that comes with your position as a leader. You want to be real and open with people, but at the same time, you want to be able to provide feedback that is helpful. The fact that there is no "one-size-fits-all" method means that not every person can or should be managed in the same way. Different individuals have unique needs and preferences when it comes to leadership styles. Being adaptable and understanding each team member's strengths and weaknesses can help you tailor your approach to effectively motivate and guide them. By striking the right balance between authority and approachability, you can foster a positive and productive work environment that encourages collaboration and trust among team members.

An effective leader recognises that they need to be adaptable and flexible in their approach to get the best out of the unique individuals on their team. Leadership is about people, not power. As leaders, we must be accessible, approachable, and authentic. This means actively listening to our team members and valuing their input and ideas. By being open and receptive to their thoughts and concerns, we can foster a culture of transparency and inclusivity. Additionally, a leader should lead by example and demonstrate the behaviours and values they expect from their team. Through consistent communication, support, and recognition, an effective leader can inspire their team to reach their full potential and achieve success together.

If we want to create a thriving culture, we must become an example of what this looks like through deeds rather than words alone. For example, a sales leader who values transparency could implement regular feedback meetings where team members are encouraged to ask questions and share their thoughts openly. This creates a safe space for honest communication and shows that the leader is open to feedback and willing to address concerns. Additionally, the sales leader could establish a mentorship programme where senior executives mentor junior employees, promoting inclusivity and creating opportunities for growth within the organisation.

By actively demonstrating these behaviours, the leader sets a precedent for others to follow and helps foster a culture of Teams need to also remember that nobody is perfect and that their leader will be subject to making mistakes. What is important is that leaders and team members learn from mistakes and communicate constructively to create a productive workplace.

Chapter 2: Team Dynamics and Communication

Effective Communication

How important is it for leaders to communicate clearly? Clear communication is essential in leadership as it ensures that team members understand their roles and responsibilities, goals, and expectations. It helps to minimise misunderstandings, conflicts, and errors. Additionally, clear communication promotes transparency and trust within the team, allowing for open dialogue and effective problem-solving.

In the modern world of business, the methods of communication, the pace of communication, and the sheer volume of information can be extremely daunting. Just take into consideration a typical working week. Things that were already difficult before the pandemic have become considerably more difficult as a result of it. Because many sales teams now operate in a hybrid environment or remotely, it is imperative that you communicate in a way that is both clear and intentional.

New sales leaders are also required to communicate effectively. They need to provide regular updates and reports to their superiors, ensuring that important information is conveyed accurately and efficiently. Additionally, effective communication with higher management helps establish trust and fosters a collaborative working environment, leading to better decision-making and overall success for the sales team. For example, a new sales leader may need to present their team's sales projections and performance data during a virtual board meeting. They must effectively communicate the challenges their team faces in the remote setting, propose innovative solutions, and demonstrate the impact of their strategies on overall revenue growth. This requires clear and intentional communication to ensure alignment and support from senior management in driving successful sales outcomes.

The Harvard Business Review identifies proficiency in oral and written communication as two of the top six characteristics of effective executives. When it comes to connecting with your sales staff, the "coach approach" is the most effective strategy for sales leaders to use.

The coach's method emphasises the development of both strategic and tactical skills. As the leader of the sales team, it is your responsibility to encourage the members of your sales team to think strategically and to look ahead one year. In addition to this, they need to give some thought to the strategic adjustments that they need to make on a daily, weekly, and monthly basis in order to meet their sales quotas.

Ideas for fostering open communication within the team

There is more than one way your team communicates. You must know all five forms of communication if you hope to build a high-performing team. Use this outline to identify areas of communication where your team can improve.

Verbal communication:

The most significant point of connection between members of a team is the communication that takes place verbally. Conversations among the members of your team, whether they take place in person, over the phone, or through video conferencing, have the potential to be the deciding factor in how each person regards the others. Communication that takes place verbally affords individuals in a team the greatest opportunity to voice their opinions.

Nonverbal communication: Body language, facial expressions, and tone of voice are all examples of what are considered to fall under the category of nonverbal communication. A great number of individuals are unaware of the impact that nonverbal communication has on the connections they have. However, the fact that more than half of all communication is nonverbal demonstrates why it is essential to pay attention to messages that aren't being said.

Written communication:

When you put your thoughts down on paper, you have greater control over how you express yourself. Your group ought to have a unified objective of achieving successful communication across all textual communication channels, be they emails, tools for project management, messaging, or reviews. Your team and your audience will both gain if you are able to effectively communicate through the medium of writing.

Visual communication:

When you're sharing information with your team through slides or videos at a meeting or training session, it's crucial to prioritise visual communication. One advantage of using pictures is that they give you some thinking time before you have to deliver your idea to other people. Think about whether or not the graphics you've chosen will make what you're attempting to communicate to your team easier for them to understand before you share them.

Listening:

You may not think of listening as communicating, but successful communication can't occur without it. When other people talk to you, you can pick up information by listening to what they say. Particularly, engaging in active listening helps to foster a positive and productive atmosphere at work because it demonstrates to the speaker that you are interested in and paying attention to what they have to say.

Six strategies to build team communication skills

There are many approaches that may be taken to enhance the communication that occurs within a team while at work. These action steps will enhance team collaboration and develop healthy connections, regardless of position or rank, whether your team works remotely or in the office. This is the case whether or not your team works in the office.

1. Speedy resolution of conflicts

Conflicts at work can begin at a low level and appear to be unimportant at first. One team member might, for example, take actions that hinder the group from accomplishing its goals, which would put more pressure on the other members of the group to perform well for the group. This in itself could lead to some form of conflict within the team. However, if the team has established effective communication and collaboration practices, they can quickly address this conflict by openly discussing their concerns and finding a solution that works for all parties. This not only prevents the conflict from escalating but also ensures that the team's achievement of their goals stays on track and deadlines are met efficiently.

After the initial member of the team has apologised to the other members, everything appears to be in order. If the original team member continues to exhibit unacceptable behaviour and the rest of the team has not explained how the change affects their work, the rest of the team may develop feelings of resentment and frustration. When members of a team do not immediately resolve problems, stress builds up, which in turn negatively impacts work performance.

Tip: Teach conflict resolution skills to team members so they can handle concerns quickly, directly, and respectfully. This prevents minor issues from becoming major ones.

2. Encourage engagement.

Although no one likes the feeling of being micromanaged, members of a team may report a lack of involvement in the absence of clear direction or collaborative efforts from the group. As a manager, it is essential to motivate members of the team while at the same time allowing them the autonomy to exercise their creative faculties.

For example, a manager could encourage engagement by regularly scheduling team meetings where everyone has the opportunity to contribute ideas and provide updates on their projects. This creates a sense of inclusivity and allows team members to feel heard and valued in the decision-making process. Additionally, the manager can establish channels for open communication, such as a shared online platform or regular check-ins, to ensure that everyone feels involved and informed about the progress of different tasks within the team.

Try holding weekly meetings or brainstorming sessions with your team in order to share knowledge and ideas with one another. Keep in mind that it is not enough to simply ask your staff for ideas; you must also demonstrate that you value each concept. The members of the team will feel more at ease knowing that they have your backing.

Tip: Schedule weekly meetings so everyone can share what they're working on and ask questions if necessary. Meetings are a great way to engage your team without interrupting important focus time.

3. Promote bottom-up communication.

It's possible that the team members at the bottom of the team hierarchy won't feel comfortable speaking out and offering their views. When you support communication from the bottom up, you encourage people on the team in every position to contribute ideas and convey their perspectives. You may encourage this kind of communication with your team by working to develop trust and morale among members of the group and providing them with a sense of ownership in the initiatives.

In a team that values open lines of communication, a lower-level team member may feel safe voicing suggestions for improving efficiency. With this information, the group as a whole may be able to save a lot of money and work much more efficiently. In addition, the team's morale and job satisfaction may increase as a result of being actively involved in decision-making processes and having their input valued.

Tip: Team members may need a boost if you want them to feel comfortable speaking up. Ask them for their ideas, opinions, and feedback so they get used to sharing. Encourage team members in different environments, like team meetings, surveys, one-on-one interactions, and a suggestion box format.

4. Aim for transparency.

team members that value open communication and are committed to maintaining it in the workplace. If you and your team members can be honest with one another, then you'll lessen the potential for miscommunication and any hazards that come with it.

Being truthful about the performance of the team and disclosing information as it happens are two ways that a leader can demonstrate transparency. In addition, whenever you believe it is necessary, you should offer your team members some form of constructive criticism so that they can develop their talents. Most importantly, it is essential to relate their day-to-day work to the larger aims of the organisation. Motivating team members and making them feel like valuable contributors to the team can be accomplished by providing them with context for their job and demonstrating the significance of the work they do.

Tip: Being open and honest is not the same as giving too much. For instance, it's helpful for your team to know if they met their annual sales goals, but you don't need to talk about the personal problems you had with the CEO this week.

5. Schedule one-on-one meetings.

Team communication takes place in both group settings and individual interactions. When team members communicate, they contribute energy from their individual experiences back to the group. Regular one-on-one meetings allow you to resolve issues and check in on your team members' well-being. When you give your team the freedom to speak openly, they will feel more confident. You can also urge your team members to meet one-on-one so they can get to know one another and create collaborative relationships.

Tip: As a manager, you don't have to be a therapist, but you should be concerned about how your team members are doing. If a team member is experiencing emotional distress, see if you can give them time off so they can return to work in a better state."

6. Consistently provide feedback.

Feedback on performance is an essential component of communication within a team. In order to maintain their motivation and level of engagement, members of the team require regular feedback on how they are performing. During your one-on-one sessions with team members, it is important to provide feedback and address areas for improvement. You might also inquire with other members of the team to see if they have any input for you.

Tip: Team members may not always feel comfortable giving you direct feedback. Consider distributing an anonymous survey so you can get honest opinions from your team on your performance as team leader.

Team Building and Motivation

The ability to motivate salespeople is an essential component of any successful organisation. It is a term that refers to the methods and approaches that companies implement in order to motivate their sales staff to perform to the best of their abilities and meet their goals. Highly motivated sales teams often outperform those who aren't driven in any way, shape, or form. This can be accomplished through defining goals, participating in incentive programmes, receiving training, or being acknowledged. Because they are constantly exposed to intense pressure and must compete with other sellers, salespeople require a significant amount of motivation. In addition to this, inspiring sales teams typically results in enhanced job satisfaction, improved morale, and a more upbeat and productive culture inside the organisation.

Individual factors are important considerations in determining how effectively a sales team can be motivated to achieve the desired results. Personality characteristics, levels of motivation, and skills and abilities are all examples of these determinants. Personality traits are a significant factor in defining the manner in which sales professionals behave, the way they think, and the way they think about their work. Through the use of behavioural assessments, managers should determine the personalities of the sales representatives in their employ and provide them with responsibilities that are tailored to their natural tendencies.

When it comes to driving sales performance, motivation is another important aspect, and one that is frequently tied to rewards and incentives. Incentives such as bonuses and perks can be effective in motivating salespeople to improve their performance; however, the nature of the reward should be tailored to the salesperson's unique requirements, qualities, and objectives.

In terms of their skills and capabilities, the members of the sales team need to have the necessary expertise, knowledge, and experience, and the organisation needs to provide frequent training to help improve their competencies.

Therefore, sales leaders must understand the personality traits of their sales representatives, set attainable goals, and provide them with the support they need to achieve success.

Every business should make it a top priority to address the organisational issues that play a role in determining the level of motivation exhibited by its sales staff. The leadership style, the culture of the firm, the salary and awards, as well as the opportunity for professional development, are all included in these considerations. A salesperson's leadership style can have an impact on both their level of motivation and their level of productivity.

It is highly likely that a leader who is able to inspire and motivate their sales team will witness an increase in employee happiness, which will ultimately lead to better sales outcomes. Examining the company culture is also an important part of the process because it can have a significant impact on employee happiness, behaviour, and overall work satisfaction. Because of the increased likelihood that personnel will be more productive and committed to the accomplishment of corporate goals, a healthy company culture can have a substantial influence on the motivation of a sales force.

Additional factors that affect the motivation of a sales force include compensation and rewards for individual salespeople. The income structure of salespeople is frequently dependent on commission, which implies that providing them with competitive compensation rates can boost their levels of motivation by providing them with a clear financial incentive to be successful in their work. In addition, certain kinds of rewards, such as bonuses or prize incentives, might inspire salespeople to make more sales than their quotas require them to do. Therefore, it is essential that the new sales leader has a comprehensive understanding of these programmes so that they can be conveyed to the team in a clear manner and so that each component can be utilised to satisfy the individual as well as the collective motivational needs of the team.

Finally, training and development opportunities for salespeople can create motivation through skill development and personal growth. When salespeople feel that they have been provided with enough training and are well-equipped to meet customer needs, they are more likely to be motivated to succeed.

A variety of external factors influence sales team motivation, which can have a positive or negative impact on sales team performance. The conditions of the market, the level of competition, and the economic variables are examples of important external elements that might have an impact on the levels of motivation of sales teams. Because there is a higher demand for items or services when market conditions are favourable, sales teams are likely to have a high level of motivation as a result. However, poor market conditions can contribute to low motivation levels among sales teams as they struggle to fulfil sales targets. This is because of the constant pressure they are under to make targets. In addition to this, the level of rivalry in the industry can have a considerable influence on the sales teams' levels of motivation. Lack of rivalry can lead to complacency and decreased motivation, but intense competition can motivate sales teams to perform to the best of their abilities and generate pressure on them to do so.

Strategies for Motivating Sales Teams

Setting Clear Goals and Expectations

Setting clear goals and expectations is crucial to maintaining a highly motivated sales team. When goals and expectations are not communicated effectively, sales representatives may lack direction and motivation, which can negatively impact their performance.

Therefore, it is important to set SMART goals (i.e., specific, measurable, attainable, relevant, and time-bound) that align with the company's overall objectives and mission. By setting these goals, sales representatives have a clear understanding of what is expected of them and are able to work towards achieving these objectives.

Additionally, it is important to clearly communicate expectations regarding sales quotas, performance metrics, and deadlines. This helps sales representatives prioritise their workload and understand what is required of them in order to meet expectations. By providing clear guidance and feedback on how to achieve these expectations, sales representatives can feel more confident in their work and motivated to reach their goals.

In order to ensure that goals and expectations are being met, it is important to monitor progress and provide ongoing feedback. Regular check-ins and performance evaluations can help sales representatives identify areas where they are excelling and areas where they may need additional support. This feedback can help sales representatives improve their performance and stay focused on achieving their goals.

Providing Feedback and Recognition

Providing feedback and recognition to sales teams is critical to their motivation and productivity. By giving feedback, you show your team that you value their efforts and that their work matters. Feedback helps them understand their strengths and weaknesses and how to improve.

It also helps teams understand what is expected of them and what they need to do to achieve their goals. Recognition, on the other hand, reinforces positive behaviour and creates a positive work environment. It lets employees know that their hard work is appreciated and encourages them to continue doing their best.

Recognition can come in various forms, such as verbal praise, certificates, awards, or promotions. However, it is essential to note that recognition should not be given randomly. It should be based on measurable results, such as meeting sales targets or improving customer satisfaction scores.

On the other hand, recognition should be timely and meaningful. It should be given when the achievement is still fresh and relevant. It should also be something that the team values, such as public recognition, an opportunity for growth, or increased compensation.

Feedback and recognition should be individualized and tailored to each team member's needs and preferences. Different people respond to different types of feedback and recognition. For instance, some may prefer public recognition, while others may prefer a private discussion.

In conclusion, providing regular and consistent feedback and recognition is essential to motivating sales teams. By doing so, you show your team that you value their work, give them direction, and create a positive work environment that encourages and rewards high performance. It is crucial to provide feedback and recognition that is specific, actionable, timely, and tailored to each team member's preferences.

Doing so will help you create a high-performing team that consistently achieves its goals.

Creating a Positive Work Environment

The work environment has a profound impact on the motivation and productivity of sales teams. Creating a positive work environment can result in higher engagement levels and increased job satisfaction, leading to better sales performance. A positive work environment can be built by offering employees opportunities for growth, encouraging open and honest communication, and promoting a sense of belonging. One effective way to create a positive work environment is by promoting work-life balance.

Sales teams are often under high levels of stress and pressure, which can lead to burnout and decreased morale. By offering flexible schedules, telecommuting options, and paid time off, employers can show that they value the well-being of their employees and prioritise work-life balance. Employers can also foster a positive work environment by promoting a culture of transparency and accountability.

By providing sales reps with clear goals and expectations, regular feedback and recognition, and opportunities for professional development, employers can create a culture of trust and collaboration. Sales reps who feel supported and valued by their employers are more likely to be motivated and productive, resulting in higher sales performance.

Offering Incentives and Rewards

The use of incentives and rewards is an effective technique that can motivate field sales teams to give their best efforts. As a sales manager, it is important to offer rewards and incentives to recognize and appreciate the team's hard work and accomplishments. Incentives can range from monetary bonuses, recognition awards, additional time off, and promotions. These incentives create a competitive environment that inspires team members to work harder to reach the set goals and achieve the set expectations.

Additionally, a well-designed sense of progression, such as longer-term promotions, paid training or mentoring, or opening relationship networks, also boosts individual satisfaction while encouraging and, therefore, sustaining targeted performance goals across the duration of the programme and the lifecycle of each sales plan.

Also, utilising formal and informal ways to encourage internal competition can energise a visceral individual contribution and magnify the collective success of the team. All types of incentives can significantly impact the work ethic, drive, and overall job satisfaction of sales team members, thereby increasing their motivation to exceed expectations and achieve the predefined goals.

Investing in Training and Development

Investing in training and development is crucial for motivating sales teams. Providing training opportunities can help employees develop their skills and knowledge, which leads to improved job satisfaction and motivation. Sales managers must ensure that they invest in the right training courses and initiatives that meet the needs of their sales teams. Managers should also design training programmes that are tailored to individual learning styles and paces.

Moreover, investing in development programmes allows salespeople to keep up with the latest industry trends and updates, which can help them stay ahead of competitors. Sales managers should provide timely training and development opportunities that equip employees with relevant skills and knowledge to perform their job roles efficiently. By investing in employee training, managers can also show their teams that they value their development and career progression, which can increase loyalty and motivation levels.

As well as formal training programmes, sales managers may also consider providing coaching and mentoring to their teams. Coaching can help employees develop their skills faster, improve their confidence, and develop a positive attitude towards their job roles. Mentoring also allows employees to learn from senior team members, which helps to build strong relationships and supports knowledge-sharing within the team.

Encouraging Collaboration and Teamwork

Encouraging collaboration and teamwork is vital to motivating sales teams. Sales is a team effort, and salespeople need to work together to achieve common goals. Collaboration unleashes creativity, different perspectives, and varied problem-solving methods. Encouraging teamwork builds a sense of togetherness and unity within the sales team, reducing conflict and competition, which can negatively impact sales performance.

Sales managers can foster teamwork by creating opportunities for salespeople to work together. For example, the manager could establish team-selling initiatives, where two or more salespeople collaborate to close a deal, or assign group projects that involve different aspects of the sales process. Salespeople could also share best practices and insights that have been effective in their previous sales experiences.

The manager could organize brainstorming sessions, where salespeople are encouraged to share creative sales strategies and tactics unique to their personality and approach. To encourage collaboration and teamwork, the sales team manager should also establish clear, measurable goals that are aligned with the sales team's vision and objectives. When salespeople can see how their efforts contribute to the team's success, they are more likely to work collaboratively to achieve those goals.

Challenges in Motivating Sales Teams

It is also critical for the new sales leader to understand that things will not be easy and that they will face numerous hurdles in their efforts to encourage their team. Some of the challenges in motivating sales teams include dealing with individual differences and personalities within the team, overcoming resistance to change, and managing conflicts that may arise. Additionally, salespeople may also face rejection and disappointment in their day-to-day activities, which can impact their motivation.

It is critical that the new sales leader develop ways to overcome these problems and support their team members. The sales leader may help sustain high levels of enthusiasm and drive within the sales team by building a good and inclusive work environment, providing continual training and development opportunities, and rewarding individual achievements.

However, with effective communication, support, and recognition, a sales leader can navigate these challenges and create a positive and motivated team environment.

Let us explore some of the challenges the new sales leader may encounter in his new role.

Resistance to Change

Resistance to change is a regular challenge that sales leaders encounter whenever they attempt to introduce new tactics or methods. When new sales efforts are implemented, it has the potential to shake up the established routine of sales teams, which frequently results in resistance. This may take the form of an unwillingness to adopt new tactics or a dismissal of the validity of new ideas.

Resistance can be the consequence of a number of different factors, including a desire to keep things as they are, a fear of failing, or an inability to adjust to changing circumstances. In order to overcome resistance to change, good communication must take place amongst team members, member participation must be encouraged, and input must be listened to. In order for sales leaders to successfully persuade sales staff to accept change, the first step is for the leader to address any underlying reluctance. One method for accomplishing this goal is to cultivate a culture of open communication among the team members so that they are at ease when addressing their issues and suggestions.

Regular team-building activities and training sessions can also increase team cohesion and foster a sense of shared purpose. Similarly, providing employees with clear goals and a pathway to achieving them can help to build a sense of ownership and investment in the success of the team.

Lack of Trust and Communication

When there are many things that can go in the way of productivity and slow down growth, it can be a daunting endeavour for any leader to try to motivate their sales team. A lack of trust and communication among members of the sales team is one of the most fundamental obstacles that sales managers must overcome. It is possible for employees to develop feelings of animosity and disengagement from their work when they believe that their ideas and opinions are not being taken into consideration or that they are not being listened to.

Additionally, there is a possibility that sales reps do not trust either their coworkers or management, which results in them working in isolation and hinders collaboration. It can be difficult for sales teams to effectively cooperate towards a common goal if the communication channels they use are not open and transparent.

In order to successfully address these problems, leaders of sales teams should work to build trust among their employees and improve communication. Open communication and the ability to provide constructive criticism can be facilitated by holding regular team meetings as well as one-on-one feedback sessions with individual members of the team.

Sales managers have a responsibility to their staff to listen attentively and empathically, noting their complaints and considering their recommendations for ways to improve. By providing members of the team with a psychologically secure environment, they will feel more at ease when it comes to sharing their thoughts and opinions, which will result in increased creativity and improved solutions. It is of the utmost importance to develop a culture of feedback and continual improvement, one in which the contributions of each member of the team are valued.

To build trust, leaders must lead by example and demonstrate the behaviour they expect from their team members. This includes setting clear expectations and following through on commitments, being transparent and honest in communication, and providing support and resources when needed. Leaders can also foster a sense of community and belonging within the team by prioritising team-building activities and encouraging socialisation outside of work.

Burnout and Stress

Burnout and stress are two main factors that can have a negative impact on the performance of a sales force. The job of a salesperson can be one of the most stressful jobs out there because many salespeople are required to work long hours and are under continual pressure to fulfil their quotas and close deals. It is highly likely that sales teams will struggle with low morale and decreased production if they fail to address burnout and stress among their team members. Apathy towards one's work, physical exhaustion, and emotional exhaustion are only a few of the signs that one may be suffering from burnout.

This can result in a reduction in motivation and engagement, which, in turn, can have a detrimental impact on the performance of the team. The promotion of a work-life balance and the encouragement of team members to take breaks and time off can be an effective way for sales managers to help reduce burnout and stress. They may also be able to provide services for the management of stress and assistance for mental health, such as access to counselling or therapy.

In addition, sales managers can enhance the morale of their teams and promote a sense of success and purpose by instituting a recognition and incentive programme for their employees. These recognition and incentive programmes do not always have to come in the form of monetary awards. For example, sales managers can implement a monthly "Top Performer" award, where the team member who achieves the highest sales targets receives public recognition and a special parking spot for the month. This non-monetary incentive not only acknowledges and motivates high performance but also fosters a positive and competitive team culture, reducing burnout and stress.

It is possible for sales managers to help assure the continued motivation and performance of their teams over the long term by placing a priority on the health and happiness of the members of their sales teams and by cultivating a positive work environment.

High Turnover Rates

A significant obstacle for sales teams, high turnover rates can result in lost productivity, the loss of valuable individuals, and increased expenditures associated with employing new staff members. One of the key variables that contributes to high employee turnover rates is a lack of job satisfaction among employees. Unachievable sales goals, insufficient job security, and a lack of opportunities for career advancement are just a few of the factors that can contribute to this dissatisfaction.

Employees who do not feel appreciated or fulfilled in their work are more likely to look for possibilities elsewhere, which is why it is essential for sales managers to cultivate an atmosphere that is supportive of their employees and offers incentives to encourage retention.

The practice of providing regular feedback and acknowledgment to employees is one strategy to improve employee happiness and lower turnover rates. The ability of managers to boost employee morale and instill a sense of shared purpose within a team can be accomplished through the provision of constructive criticism to workers as well as public acknowledgment of their accomplishments.

Chapter 3: Performance Management

This is perhaps the most difficult area for many newly promoted sales leaders, according to my observations and findings. As a result of the fact that performance management is dependent on so many different aspects of a leader's skill set, it is perhaps the area that could pose the greatest difficulty to a rookie leader who has not yet refined all of these talents.

In order to effectively manage performance, sales leaders must possess a strong understanding of goal-setting, performance evaluation, and providing feedback. These skills are crucial for creating a culture of continuous improvement and ensuring that team members are motivated and aligned with organisational objectives. Additionally, regular communication and coaching sessions can help sales leaders identify areas for improvement and provide the necessary support to help their team members succeed.

I have encountered misunderstandings regarding the purpose of performance management and its components. The majority of the time, sales leaders are more at ease when dealing with high-performing salespeople, but they can find it tough to address low-performing salespeople. Because it is constantly associated with underperformance, performance management has a reputation for having a negative connotation. This is one of the reasons why.

This ought not to be the case at all. The new leader should have a solid understanding of what performance management is all about, the framework within which it operates, and the fact that its primary focus is always on improving performance and is not intended as a means of getting rid of employees who are not meeting expectations.

Setting Clear Expectations

Employees must understand what is expected of them in order to work properly. An up-to-date job description that outlines the core activities, tasks, and responsibilities of the job is the starting point. It also describes the main areas of knowledge and abilities that an individual must have in order to be effective on the job. Expectations for performance go beyond the job description. They include specific goals and targets that employees should strive to achieve. These performance expectations should be communicated clearly and regularly to employees, so they have a clear understanding of what is expected of them. By setting clear expectations, employers can establish a benchmark for measuring employee performance and identify any gaps or areas for improvement. This not only helps in managing and developing employees but also serves as a basis for evaluating their performance and making informed decisions about their future with the organisation.

When you consider high-quality on-the-job performance, you are truly considering a variety of expected job outcomes, such as An employee should understand why the position exists, where it fits in the company, and how the job's tasks link to organisational and departmental objectives when discussing performance expectations. This understanding is crucial for employees to align their efforts with the overall goals of the organisation and contribute effectively to its success. Additionally, clear performance expectations enable managers to provide constructive feedback and support employees in their professional development, ultimately leading to a more engaged and motivated workforce.

What expectations do employees have? It goes without saying that managing expectations within your team is crucial. First, though, it's important to clarify what is meant when people refer to "employee expectations." What are the precise requirements for employees? Here, "employee expectations" refers to what a leader and company anticipate from a certain person.

Employees may have expectations of their company or boss as well, but here we are focusing on what is expected of individual employees. Employee expectations are defined by a company's leadership or management team as their conduct, performance, work assignments, and outcomes. These expectations can be clearly stated in a performance contract or job description. They can also be shared more casually during team meetings or one-on-one conversations. In addition to the task itself, employee expectations typically involve how people work and interact with others. Another crucial part of setting expectations is the results or outcomes.

Do you know that businesses that set sales goals every quarter fetch 31% more returns than those who stick to annual goal setting? The main aim of a business is to earn profit and grow. To achieve that, the organization has to work collaboratively and set goals. After all, that's how you will run the show.

With sales goals, your sales team has a benchmark to achieve. It will help motivate reps to put in their best efforts. You can amplify the feeling further by providing special incentives to those who can surpass the goal. However, setting sales goals is not an easy task for sales managers, as many factors come into play. Plus, they have to be attainable and realistic. Going wrong can have a serious impact on the outcome.

So what are the sales goals? Sales goals are the sales objectives meant for the sales team of a company. To set realistic sales goals, you have to keep the skills of each team member in mind. Try to pay attention to the following while you set sales goals for your sales team:

1. Increasing sales to fetch more profits for the business

2. Increasing the productivity of sales reps

3. Indulging more in cross-selling and upselling

4. Retention of existing customers and acquiring new ones

5. Better management of time"

So what do I do now?

1. Begin setting sales goals from the bottom up.

Always begin the process of goal-setting by seeing the end result as you would like it to be. It will assist you in making decisions that are conducive to getting you there. It is simple; all you have to do is imagine where you want to go in a year's time and devise some objectives that will get you there. Just keep in mind that your objectives need to be congruent with the overarching mission of the organisation you work for. At this point, you need to place more of an emphasis on describing the outcome that you want as opposed to specific targets. You need to make a note of the conclusion that you want, and then use that outcome to guide you along the road that you should take to evaluate the goals that you establish for the future.

While you are doing this, you also provide yourself with the opportunity to get input from your team and evaluate the ability and contribution that each member of your team can make towards the accomplishment of your overall objective. Because of this engagement, your team will have a better chance of buying in and taking ownership of the overarching goals that have been established.

2. Understand the present situation.

After you have finished looking into the future, you should return to the here and now and examine the strategy, resources, and customers that you are now working with. Find out all you need in order to get to where you see yourself being in the future. You need to take into account both the here and now and the picture you have in your head of the future when you are trying to help yourself effectively develop smart sales goals.

Educate yourself on the many approaches to sales forecasting. After you have finished imagining what the future holds for you, you should return to the here and now and evaluate the strategy, resources, and customers that you currently have. Find out all you need in order to get to where you see yourself being in the future. You need to take into account both the here and now and the picture you have in your head of the future when you are trying to help yourself effectively develop smart sales goals. Educate yourself on the many approaches to sales forecasting.

3. Set SMART Goals.

When it comes to setting objectives for your sales department, the S.M.A.R.T. methodology is a good option to consider. The acronym SMART is comprised of five parts: Specific, Measurable, Attainable, Relevant, and Time-bound. These are the components that make up the acronym. It suggests that each and every one of your company's goals should incorporate these five characteristics in some way. Let's take a closer look at each one of them to get a better understanding of the situation, shall we?

Specific

As a sales leader, you should be clear about your goals for your team. If you have a goal such as growing revenue, it will not be SMART because you are not detailed. A specific target would be to increase sales by 60%. It is more definite and clearly defined because it is a tangible and measurable goal. It will assist the sales team in developing a strategy to achieve it. For example, a sales leader might set a goal for their team to increase sales by 60% within the next quarter. This specific target provides clear direction and allows the team to focus their efforts on developing strategies to achieve this growth. By having a specific goal, the sales leader can effectively track progress and make adjustments as needed to ensure success.

Measurable

A goal that can be measured is considered to be a SMART objective. You ought to be able to monitor the way things are going towards the goal. Therefore, rather than having a goal such as "increase revenue," you should have a quantitative target such as "increase revenue by 60 percent in a year." When you have a goal that can be measured, it is easy to measure the progress that your team is making towards achieving that goal.

By having a specific numerical target, you can track your team's progress and identify any areas that may need improvement. Measuring the progress of your goal allows for better accountability and ensures that everyone is working towards the same objective. Additionally, a measurable goal provides a clear benchmark for success, allowing you to celebrate achievements and make necessary adjustments along the way to ensure ultimate success.

Attainable

While setting lofty goals for your team is admirable, your representatives also need to be able to achieve them. They must be attainable by a representative through adherence to standard work ethics. Stated differently, the objectives must be reasonable. For instance, rather than encouraging the representatives to strive for 50% of the sales, you should set a goal of 25% for the following month if they can achieve a 20% growth in sales. While setting high standards for them is OK, setting unrealistic expectations for them might cause stress and disappointment if they fall short of the mark. For example, a sales team could be given the objective of increasing their customer base by 10% in the next quarter by consistently providing excellent customer service and actively seeking new leads. This goal is reasonable as it pushes the representatives to strive for growth but also takes into account the effort required to achieve it. By setting attainable goals like this, representatives can work towards success without feeling overwhelmed or discouraged.

Relevant

Your company's goals must be pertinent to your line of business. It is not worthwhile to create a goal that is unrelated to your business. Your objectives must always support the expansion of your business and align with its description. Having relevant goals ensures that representatives are focusing their efforts on areas that directly contribute to the growth and success of the company. By aligning goals with the business's description and objectives, representatives can prioritise their actions and make better decisions that will ultimately drive the company forward. This also helps in maintaining a sense of purpose and motivation among the representatives, as they can see the direct impact of their efforts on the overall success of the business. For example, a sales representative for an insurance company may have a goal to increase revenue by 20% in the next quarter. By aligning this goal with the company's objective of expanding its customer base, the representative can prioritise activities such as prospecting and lead generation, which directly contribute to acquiring new customers and increasing sales. This clear alignment not only ensures that the representative is focusing on actions that will drive growth but also provides a sense of purpose and motivation by showing them how their efforts directly impact

Time-bound

Goals for your team must have a deadline in order for you to quit putting them off. Setting time-bound goals will push you and the team to work harder and meet your sales targets on time. If there is no deadline, your team will be unmotivated to strive towards its goals. Additionally, time-bound goals create a sense of urgency and accountability within the team. Knowing that there is a specific timeframe to achieve the goals encourages individuals to prioritise tasks and stay focused on achieving results within the given time frame. This helps in maintaining productivity and driving growth effectively.

The new sales leader must also be aware of the risks of driving the time-bound part of the target erratically. While deadlines can instill a sense of urgency, they can also result in rushed and low-quality work, since the emphasis may be on reaching the deadline rather than providing the greatest possible results. Furthermore, not all people thrive under pressure and may feel overwhelmed or burned out, resulting in lower production and potentially detrimental effects on team morale.

Evaluation of Performance

As a result of my experience dealing with sales managers or representatives over their sales performance, I believe it is important to look at sales from the four perspectives listed below at all times. A new sales leader should adopt this mindset as well, because it will guarantee that his team's sales contributions are always in line with the organisation's business objectives.

The four key elements of sales performance are pretty straightforward when you look at them written out, but it is so common for business representatives, business owners, and sales managers to dwell upon total sales volume at the expense of neglecting the other three key elements. The purpose of this section is not to go into great depth on any one of the four components, but rather to emphasise how important it is to take into account all four components whenever you assess the performance of your sales team.

Sales Volume

I won't go on and on about how important it is to have enough sales in monetary terms to fulfil or surpass your business plan targets. The main idea of this piece is that regardless of overall sales volume, you cannot accurately evaluate sales performance until you carefully consider the three criteria below to grade your total sales monetary quality.

Sales Mix

Understanding your sales mix is critical, unless you just offer a single product or service. The percentage of your overall sales attributed to each product and/or service offering for your organisation is described as the sales mix. The ideal application for a pie chart is to clearly display all of your company's product sales. The profitability of an enterprise will frequently depend on the product sales mix because various goods and services typically have different gross margins.

When evaluating your sales mix, it's important to keep in mind that you need to strike a balance between your ability to manufacture the product or service and how much of it you sell. This could significantly benefit you or hurt you. So, a product that makes you a lot of money and that you can deliver to customers' satisfaction is an example of this. On the other hand, a product that is hard for you to make and that you deliver to customers for a low gross margin might not be the best way to make most of your sales.

There are other reasons why a sales mix can become out of balance that are beyond the scope of this book, but make sure your sales mix is at the forefront of any evaluation of how your sales force is functioning.

Sales Margins

It is unusual for margins to be consistent across products. You usually make a little more money on certain products than others, and the cost of goods sold varies greatly between product or service offers. In certain circumstances, the margins change regularly, requiring managers to keep track of them on a daily basis.

Your sales mix, as indicated above, may have an impact on your sales margins, but other key causes include increased costs, unfavourable sales pricing, or both. By including sales margins in any evaluation of sales performance, you increase your chances of detecting problems before they become significant and taking corrective action.

It is common for sales teams to be so focused on top-line sales as their performance indicator that they view margin as merely an operational concern; however, this is not the case.

Customer Satisfaction

The main reason customer happiness is so important is because it is difficult to measure and track. Because tracking client satisfaction is difficult, it is critical to include it in any sales success discussion. Regardless of how complex or crude your customer relationship management tool is or what type of customer survey you use, I'm a firm believer in going old-school to keep your finger on the pulse of customer happiness. If you have access to technology-driven data collection, it can be quite beneficial, but I caution against depending only on survey results or sales staff assessments.

The best and most proactive measure is the sales managers need to be talking to customers and asking them for feedback directly. "How are we doing, what would you like to see, are we meeting all your needs?"

Repeat business is the best and most accurate historical metric of consumer satisfaction. If a customer switches to a competitor after using your products or services, you must understand why. Keeping an existing customer is significantly easier and less expensive than finding a new one.

I've worked with salespeople who were excellent at finding new sales prospects but who left a path of dead bodies in their wake—that is, bodies of customers who did not want to continue buying after the original transaction was completed. If you can't count on repeat business from your present clientele, it's going to be difficult to maintain steady growth in sales.

After the sale has been completed and the goods have been delivered, the customer should be asked how they feel about the transaction overall as part of your sales performance review.

None of the information contained in these four essential components for assessing sales performance is particularly revolutionary. Motivating my creation of this section in the book was the frequency with which I observe business leaders and sales managers neglect one or more of the evaluation criteria in favour of concentrating exclusively on top-line sales. Many sellers get very frustrated when they are responsible for all four of these important parts, which is why it is even more important to stress that the salesperson is in charge of all of these duties.

If your sales team does not accept responsibility for all four of the reasons listed below, they may put you in a financially disastrous situation.

Coaching and Development

As stated multiple times throughout this book, sales coaching is one of the most critical roles of any sales leader. As a result, it goes without saying that new sales managers will need to focus and spend significant time honing their coaching skills. Sales coaching is essential for the success of the sales team, as it helps improve their performance and achieve their targets. Without proper coaching and development, sales managers may struggle to guide their team effectively, leading to missed opportunities and potential financial losses for the company. Therefore, investing time and effort in developing strong coaching skills is crucial for sales managers to ensure the overall success of the sales team.

By honing their coaching skills, sales managers can effectively identify areas for improvement for their team members and provide tailored guidance and support. This not only boosts the confidence and motivation of the sales team but also enhances their selling techniques and customer interactions. Moreover, effective coaching helps sales managers build strong relationships with their team members, fostering a positive and collaborative work environment. Ultimately, investing in sales coaching not only benefits the individual sales representatives but also contributes to the overall growth and profitability of the company.

There is a myth that only low performers need coaching. The fact is that coaching benefits all performers. For example, a high-performing sales representative who consistently meets or exceeds their targets may still benefit from coaching to refine their skills and stay ahead of market trends. Through coaching, they can learn new strategies, receive feedback on their performance, and continuously improve their selling techniques. This not only helps them maintain their success but also sets them up for continued growth and professional development within the company.

There have been numerous occasions in which sales managers have held the belief that this task falls under the purview of the department that is responsible for training and development. It may not be ingrained in your culture, but as a leader, it is your responsibility to cultivate the growth of others.

Set an example. In order to encourage others to bring their best selves to work, you should set an example. Never allow another person's lack of commitment to affect your own. Initiate a trend of sales coaching right away.

In many cases, sales managers view this role as confrontational because they are accustomed to only providing coaching to employees who are not performing up to industry standards. It is necessary for the sales leader to adopt a positive mindset during this process in order to get the most out of the person who is being coached. An effective sales coaching method is one that emphasises collaboration and constructiveness. Focus on the actions rather than the individual. Please convey your goals and objectives. Inquire about people's opinions and pay attention. Pay close attention. Have a mindset that is focused on finding solutions, and respond to obstacles with empathy. Also, discuss the positive results that result from the behaviours that are wanted.

Managers can approach the process with the constricting belief that a person has attained their maximum potential and that there is no room for improvement. The truth is that a person can always grow if they have the right beliefs and support system in place. By adopting a growth mindset, managers can encourage their team members to continuously develop and reach new heights. This involves providing constructive feedback, offering opportunities for learning and development, and fostering a culture of continuous improvement. With the right approach, managers can unlock the untapped potential within their team members and witness remarkable growth and success.

There is also the myth that there is not enough time to coach. The "tyranny of the urgent" can easily cause one to lose sight of what is actually vital in the moment. In the end, coaching gives managers a lot more time back since it gives sales teams the drive and self-assurance to tackle novel and varied scenarios. Time invested up front might pay off handsomely in the long run for astute management.

The expression "I don't have the time" frequently conceals more serious issues on the part of the sales manager, such as a lack of confidence, self-assurance, or the skills needed to complete the task successfully. For example, a sales manager who constantly says "I don't have the time" when asked to provide feedback on a sales team's performance may actually be struggling with their own ability to evaluate and coach their team effectively. This lack of confidence and skills can hinder the development and success of the sales team, leading to missed opportunities and poor performance overall. However, if the sales manager invests time in receiving coaching themselves, they can gain the necessary confidence and skills to effectively lead and guide their team.

For this reason, it is quite necessary for the sales leader to locate mentors who are able to assist them in this particular field. Newly promoted sales managers also seek opportunities to observe their colleagues who have demonstrated success in this particular component of their job. By observing successful colleagues, sales managers can learn valuable strategies and techniques that have proven effective in leading a sales team. Additionally, seeking out mentors who have experience in sales leadership can provide invaluable guidance and support, helping the manager develop the necessary skills and confidence to excel in their role.

The techniques listed below can help a new sales leader coach his or her team for better performance.

1. Sales coaches follow a formal process.

It will be easier for your sales managers and representatives to maintain consistency if you establish and adhere to a structured process. This procedure needs to be able to be demonstrated and replicated. According to research by Sandler Training, sales teams with higher levels of success were 1.4 times more likely to use a formal sales process with metrics.

2. Meet regularly with their sales teams.

In addition to being well organised, good coaches also keep a regular session schedule intact. It is possible that the first few sessions will be held closer together because both the student and the teacher are still getting used to everything. It is common practice to recommend holding meetings every two weeks because this provides the salesperson with the opportunity to put what they have learned into practice. The sales manager is also afforded the opportunity to observe and compile feedback during this period.

3. Sales managers devote time to sessions.

Although it may be tempting to add a meeting to your session in order to maximise productivity, you should resist the urge to do so. In the context of coaching, it can be a distraction. First and foremost, you should avoid having your sales representative feel overwhelmed. Give them some time to think about what they have been taught. Additionally, this will demonstrate to the salesman that you appreciate his or her time and are committed to educating them.

4. Sales managers use data.

In the end, the numbers are the best indicator of what is actually going on. The ability to gather and examine data in order to draw conclusions, as well as the ability to successfully convey those conclusions, are all essential skills for great sales coaches. In addition to providing the sales professional with a clear picture of their success, this data should also indicate the next steps that they should take.

5. Sales managers challenge teams.

Putting people through difficult situations is the only way for them to develop. If you want to benefit your team members in the long run, you should not be scared to force them out of their comfort zone for a while. They should be given a new sales approach to attempt, their quota should be increased after they reach a certain threshold, or they should begin something else that will demand them to engage in some critical thinking and physical labour.

6. Document sales performance.

Remember to take notes throughout each session so that you may keep a record of what has been discussed and what has been decided upon. Following the event, it is highly likely that your mind will not remember everything that took place. It is important for both you, as the sales manager, and the representative to do this so that they can refer back to their notes for reference.

7. Developing trust through authenticity

It is important for the greatest sales managers to admit when they have failed in the past because doing so helps to create trust in the relationship. Telling anecdotes about these occasions will have the effect of encouraging each individual and letting them realise that they are not alone. The measures that you followed to fix the problem should also be shared with them, as this will provide them with a real-life example of how to handle challenges that arise while working.

8. Have the team rate itself.

Self-evaluation helps people learn more about themselves, which can make them feel better about their work. Allow the seller to think about their work and listen to what they have to say. Have some questions ready to help them out. For instance, what were the hardest things for you this quarter? What did you do right?

9. Maintain singular focus on a single subject.

It will take some time before you notice significant gains, but it will take considerably longer if you are forcing the representative to complete an excessive number of assignments. Provide them with a single task at a time, which will not only provide them with sufficient room to concentrate but will also enable you to more accurately evaluate their progress.

10. Inspire your team effectively.

When it comes to sales coaching, successful sales coaches do more than just set targets and instruct individuals on what to do. Each individual member of the team is given the ability to make decisions and is inspired to perform to the best of their abilities by the greatest coaches. In addition to providing words of encouragement, they do this by retaining a pleasant mood and a cool composure the entire time.

11. Take a unique approach to each team member.

Given that every single person is one of a kind, it is important to take this into consideration. It is impossible to avoid unfavourable outcomes if one consistently follows the same advice and treats all individuals in the same manner. When contrasted to the other representatives, each individual will have a distinct collection of aptitudes, constraints, personalities, and preferences. Acquire this knowledge, and then modify your teaching methods to cater to the individual requirements of each student.

12. Provide sales training that has proven results.

The best coaches, whether they are in sales or sports, are able to win. A few times, they have failed, and they have made some mistakes, but here is the most important thing: they have learned from their mistakes and improved as a result of their experiences. Having real-world sales experience and being able to mentor their sales representatives in a range of situations make the best sales trainers, in my opinion. The most effective sales coaches are able to offer real-time advice on abilities such as self-awareness, people skills, and closing methods.

It is likely that the most effective sales trainers have previously put their sales strategies to the test. They are able to provide their team members with efficient sales training that accomplishes the desired objectives since they have their sales approach in hand. Review the training and methods you've received in sales. They might be absolutely right. Alternately, they can require a rework of your sales approach in order to adapt it to the post-pandemic environment and ensure that it delivers results.

13. Refer your team to additional learning resources.

Because you only have a limited amount of time in each teaching session, it is essential that you give your salespeople the authority to take responsibility for their own success. You can accomplish this by directing them to other resources that are geared to provide extra sales training. These resources may include relevant blog posts, online articles, websites, books, webinars, and other similar materials from the internet.

14. Developing a continuous learning environment

Developing a continuous learning environment is crucial for the growth and development of your sales team. Encourage them to attend workshops, seminars, and conferences that focus on sales techniques and strategies. Additionally, consider implementing regular team meetings or training sessions where salespeople can share their experiences and learn from one another. For example, you could organise a monthly sales workshop where your team can learn about new sales techniques and strategies from industry experts. This not only provides them with valuable knowledge but also encourages them to stay motivated and engaged in their work.

Additionally, you could encourage your sales team to attend relevant conferences or seminars where they can network with other professionals in the field and gain new insights into the industry. By fostering a culture of continuous learning, you can ensure that your sales team stays up-to-date with the latest industry trends and continuously improves their skills.

This commitment to ongoing education will not only benefit your sales team individually, but it will also have a positive impact on your company as a whole. When your salespeople are equipped with the latest knowledge and skills, they will be better equipped to meet the evolving needs of your customers and close more deals. Moreover, investing in their professional development shows your team that you value their growth and are committed to their success. This can boost morale and motivation, leading to increased productivity and, ultimately, higher sales numbers.

Chapter 4: Sales Strategy and Planning

Strategic Thinking

While your new work is primarily focused on coaching and training your sales team to continuously meet and exceed sales goals, which is highly operationally intensive, it is critical for sales managers to also embrace a strategic thinking approach. Some regard this position as less strategic because the sales manager's job is to push and achieve the company's objectives, which he or she has been briefed on. I respectfully disagree, since how you deploy your team in the market, how the team responds to rival activity in that area, and how you deploy the right seller for the right markets take a lot of thought at the sales manager level. These are just a few areas where strategic thinking is essential.

In addition to these aspects, a sales manager's strategic thinking also comes into play when setting sales targets and forecasting future sales. It is not just about pushing for immediate results but also about analysing market trends, identifying potential opportunities, and making informed decisions that will drive long-term success. By taking a strategic approach, a sales manager can effectively allocate resources, identify areas for improvement, and develop innovative strategies to stay ahead of the competition. This level of thinking requires a deep understanding of the market, the company's strengths and weaknesses, and the ability to adapt to changing dynamics. It is a role that requires a combination of analytical skills, leadership abilities, and strong communication skills. The sales manager must be able to effectively communicate the company's value proposition to potential clients and motivate their team to achieve sales targets. Additionally, they must stay updated on industry trends and competitor activities in order to anticipate market shifts and adjust their strategies accordingly. Overall, being a successful sales manager entails not only managing a team but also being a strategic thinker who can drive the company's growth and success in the long run.

As a result, how can you, as a new employee in this role, prepare yourself to deal with this particular facet of your work expectations? Let's begin with the most important item.

1. Establish a strategic foundation for your sales force.

Once you have freed yourself from the demands of operational labour, you will have the opportunity to engage in strategic work. In order to accomplish this, you must first disengage yourself from the role of mercenary closer. You should let the sellers handle the sale. To ensure that they are successful in their profession of selling, provide them with every conceivable tool. This includes thorough product knowledge, efficient sales training, and continuing assistance. By empowering sellers to perform their jobs, you can focus on the broader picture and contribute to the organisation's overall growth and success. Remember, as a strategic thinker and leader, your responsibility is to guide and mentor, not to micromanage. Believe in your team's abilities and equip them with the resources they require to thrive. By completely preparing sellers for the long-term success that they can achieve on their own, you will free yourself to take a more strategic approach. This is where the multiplication impact occurs. The better your sellers are equipped, the more strategic you can be. And the more you can do strategically, the more equipped your sellers will be for peak performance.

Engage in a discussion regarding the vision, mission, and purpose of your job. It is important to keep in mind that your professional position requires you to concurrently manage sales and lead people. For the purpose of motivating salespeople, your leadership is essential. Inspiration does not originate from the mundane, routine, and ordinary actions that are performed on a daily basis and are repeated. This information is not included in the management check-ins that ask, "What have you done for me recently?" Because reaching sales goals is an integral part of a seller's routine, there is no connection between this and the achievement of targets. In order to motivate sellers, it is necessary to consider the bigger picture.

2. Develop your strategic thinking skills.

Being strategic doesn't happen automatically. In addition to overcoming all the conditioning you've had for focusing on tactics, you're going to need new skills to go along with your new perspective. It takes practice to master any new skill. You won't be good at it right from the start, even if you have natural tendencies toward strategic planning and thinking. Strategic thinking is crucial for a new sales manager to navigate the complexities of the role and contribute to the long-term success of the sales team and the organization. Here are key strategic thinking skills that a new sales manager must develop:

Visionary Planning: Develop the ability to envision the future of the sales team and align it with the overall organisational goals. This involves setting a clear direction and creating a roadmap for success.

Market Insight: Stay informed about industry trends, market dynamics, and competitor activities. A sales manager needs to understand the external factors that may impact the sales strategy and adjust plans accordingly.

Data Analysis: Master the skill of analysing data to derive meaningful insights. Utilise metrics and key performance indicators (KPIs) to assess the effectiveness of sales strategies and make data-driven decisions.

Risk Assessment: Identify potential risks and challenges in the sales landscape. Develop contingency plans and mitigation strategies to address uncertainties that may impact sales performance.

Adaptability: Cultivate flexibility in thinking and the ability to adapt to changing circumstances. A strategic sales manager should be agile in adjusting plans based on market shifts, emerging opportunities, or unforeseen challenges.

Resource Allocation: Efficiently allocate resources, including budget, time, and personnel, to maximise the impact of sales initiatives. This involves prioritising efforts based on strategic goals.

Collaboration and Communication: Foster a collaborative environment and effectively communicate the sales strategy to the team. Ensure alignment between the sales strategy and the broader organisational objectives.

Long-Term Perspective: Develop the ability to balance short-term goals with long-term objectives. This involves making decisions that not only address immediate challenges but also contribute to sustainable success over time.

Innovative Thinking: Encourage creative thinking within the sales team. Seek innovative solutions to challenges and explore new approaches to sales processes, customer engagement, and market positioning.

Customer-Centric Focus: Align strategic thinking with a deep understanding of customer needs and preferences. Develop strategies that enhance the customer experience and build long-lasting relationships.

By honing these strategic thinking skills, a new sales manager can navigate the dynamic landscape of sales management with confidence and contribute to the overall success of the team and organisation.

Any one of those bulleted items can consume time and effort just to learn. Don't let that be a barrier. Investing time to learn, practice, and perfect these skills will make you more effective as a sales manager AND set you up nicely for next-level roles.

3. Stay Focused on Strategy vs. Tactics

If you continue to revert to tactical work and thinking in the near term, the things that we are presenting here will never come to pass. In the event that you are addicted to the feeling of adrenaline that comes from putting out flames, it is highly doubtful that you will be successful in becoming more strategic. You will never be able to free yourself up to engage in activity that is of a higher level than selling if you are unable to trust your sellers with the responsibility of making significant sales. You will never be able to escape the tactical chase of this period's revenue objective if you do not invest time in coaching and educating sellers to solve difficulties and make sales with confidence.

It all boils down to becoming more proactive and less reactive. more long-term and less short-term...

To move away from short-term, reactionary responses, consider this:

"It is better to have a hen tomorrow than an egg today."– Thomas Fuller

You've been under pressure from sales to create today's egg. Now is the opportunity to think differently and care for the chicken that will lay more eggs tomorrow, next month, and next year.

Changing one's way of thinking is necessary in order to be proactive and to concentrate on the chicken. The formation of new routines requires time. You will need to retrain yourself to ask questions that are different from the ones you normally ask. Instead of wondering "What could go wrong today?" and "What do I need to fix right now?" shift to asking "What can we create that will be right in the future?" and "How can we make things better in the future than they are right now?"

When you are proactive, you are actively shaping the events and results that occur in your life. Rather than sitting around and passively reacting to events as they occur, you take action. You take measures to prepare for, intervene with, and control situations or occurrences that are anticipated. You are not at the mercy of whatever may occur since you are expecting and maintaining control of the situation. Being proactive allows you to be more prepared and confident in handling challenges that may arise. It also gives you the opportunity to make improvements and find solutions, rather than simply accepting things as they are. By taking proactive steps, you can create a better future by actively working towards positive outcomes and avoiding potential problems.

The fact that you are thinking strategically, preparing ahead, and anticipating change gives you the ability to take control of the situation. You have adequately prepared sellers to deal with any issues that may arise. No longer is it necessary for you to don your superhero cape and come to their rescue in order to save the day. You have faith in them, and you are aware that they are gaining self-awareness and maturing as they deal with these challenges. (Don't forget, once upon a time someone trusted you this way even though you weren't entirely ready and solidly proven!).

By itself, it is a form of self-discipline to recognise when you are engaging in tactical behaviour and to refuse to proceed with it. You are going to encounter some blunders, and when you do, you will need to get back on course. As time goes on, you will become more adept at identifying the strategic traps and temptations that you encounter. You will get to your destination more quickly if you place value on being strategic.

Getting some assistance is something you should think about doing as you continue to develop into the strategic sales manager you want to be. Find someone who has already accomplished this and is successful. Engage the services of a certified executive coach, who can assist you in overcoming obstacles and developing organisational responsibilities. Remember to keep studying, and even if it feels like a battle, you shouldn't give up.

Sales Planning and Forecasting: Navigating the Path to Success

As a newly appointed sales manager, the art of sales planning and forecasting becomes your compass in navigating the dynamic and competitive landscape of the business world.

Effectively charting a course for your sales team requires a strategic approach, clear objectives, and a keen understanding of market dynamics. In this article, we'll explore the fundamentals of sales planning and delve into strategies for accurate sales forecasting, equipping you with the tools to steer your team towards success.

1. Understanding the Sales Landscape

Sales planning is not merely a checklist of tasks; it's a strategic roadmap that aligns your team's efforts with the broader goals of the organisation. Begin by understanding the intricate dance between your product or service and the ever-evolving needs of your target audience. Define your objectives with precision, ensuring they resonate with the overarching business strategy. In essence, effective sales planning is about crafting a narrative that weaves seamlessly into the fabric of your company's mission.

This narrative should not only outline the specific sales targets and milestones but also provide a clear understanding of how these objectives contribute to the overall growth and success of the organisation. It requires a deep understanding of the market dynamics, the competitive landscape, and customer needs and preferences to craft a sales plan that is both realistic and ambitious. By aligning your team's efforts with the broader goals of the organisation, you can create a sense of purpose and direction that drives motivation and productivity. Furthermore, effective sales planning involves regular monitoring and evaluation to ensure that the plan remains relevant and adaptable in a rapidly changing business environment.

For example, a successful sales plan for a life assurance company may involve conducting extensive market research to identify emerging market trends and customer demands in your earmarked geographical area of operation. This could include analysing data on consumer preferences, competitor strategies, and industry forecasts. Based on this information, the sales team can then develop a realistic yet ambitious plan that aligns with the organisation's goals, such as targeting specific customer segments or expanding into new markets. Through regular monitoring and evaluation of key performance indicators, the team can make necessary adjustments to their strategy to stay ahead.

2. Setting Clear Objectives

When it comes to your sales team, having clear objectives is like having guiding lights. Specific, quantifiable, attainable, relevant, and time-bound are the acronyms that should be used to describe these objectives. Consider the possibility of setting a goal to increase sales revenue by a specific percentage over a predetermined period of time. These goals not only point you in the right direction, but they also allow you to set benchmarks for success, which enables you to evaluate your progress and make adjustments to your methods as required.

Earlier in the book, when we were talking about how to set SMART targets, we actually addressed this issue as well. Despite the fact that I advocated for the utilisation of the bottom-up strategy, it is unavoidable that your team will be assigned a target. When you are engaging your team in the bottom-up goal-setting technique, let this assigned target serve as a benchmark for you to use. It is possible to make use of this benchmark in order to direct the process in the appropriate direction, either to meet the company allotted or to exceed it in the event that the engagement leads to a higher objective. Additionally, effective sales leaders have embraced the habit of stretching the company's allotted target in the hope that this will accommodate any possibility of the team falling short of its designated goals.

By setting this assigned target as a benchmark, sales leaders can effectively guide the team towards achieving the company's goals. This benchmark serves as a reference point to measure progress and determine whether the team is on track or needs to make adjustments. Moreover, by exceeding the assigned target, sales leaders can inspire and motivate their team to strive for even greater success. This mindset of constantly pushing boundaries and stretching targets fosters a culture of continuous improvement and ensures that the team is always aiming for excellence.

Maintaining adherence to the SMART goal-setting standards during this entire process is essential. SMART goal-setting standards help to ensure that goals are specific, measurable, attainable, relevant, and time-bound. By following these standards, sales leaders can set clear expectations and track progress effectively. This not only helps in monitoring the team's performance but also allows for necessary adjustments to be made if the goals are not being achieved. Adhering to the SMART goalsetting standards also promotes transparency and accountability within the team, as everyone is aware of the specific targets and timelines they need to meet.

3. Customer-Centric Approach

Sales planning is most potent when it is rooted in a deep understanding of your customers. Take a customer-centric approach by segmenting your target audience based on demographics, behaviour, or other relevant factors. Tailor your sales plans to address the specific needs and preferences of each segment, ensuring that your approach resonates and adds value. This will help you build stronger relationships with your customers and increase their satisfaction with your products or services. By understanding their needs and preferences, you can offer personalised solutions and recommendations, ultimately leading to higher sales conversions. Additionally, a customer-centric approach helps in identifying opportunities for upselling or cross-selling, allowing you to maximise your revenue potential.

Consider a consumer who has acquired a policy from a life assurance company. A customer-centric strategy allows the company to acquire information about the customer's needs and financial status, such as affordability, in order to offer the best solution to satisfy the customer's needs. This personalised recommendation not only increases the customer's satisfaction but also leads to additional sales and revenue for the store. It is also possible for the company to proactively reach out to customers with new product offerings or updates if they remain alert to the changing needs of their customers. This will further broaden the company's revenue potential across fluctuations in demand.

4. SWOT Analysis for Sales

A SWOT analysis (Strengths, Weaknesses, Opportunities, and Threats) is a powerful tool for sales planning. Identify your team's strengths, such as a robust product offering or a highly skilled sales force. Acknowledge weaknesses, such as gaps in product knowledge or potential market challenges. Explore opportunities, such as emerging trends or untapped markets, and be vigilant about potential threats that could derail your sales objectives. By conducting a SWOT analysis, sales teams can gain a comprehensive understanding of their position in the market and make informed decisions.

This analysis allows them to leverage their strengths to gain a competitive advantage, address and improve upon their weaknesses, capitalise on opportunities for growth, and mitigate potential threats. By regularly reviewing and updating the SWOT analysis, sales teams can adapt their strategies to align with market dynamics and ensure continued success in achieving their sales objectives.

What is a SWOT analysis?

SWOT analysis is a framework for identifying and analysing an organisation's strengths, weaknesses, opportunities, and threats. These words make up the SWOT acronym.

The primary goal of SWOT analysis is to increase awareness of the factors that go into making a business decision or establishing a business strategy. To do this, SWOT analyses the internal and external environment and the factors that can impact the viability of a decision.

Businesses frequently use SWOT analysis, but nonprofit organisations and, to a lesser extent, individuals also use it for personal assessment. SWOT is also used to assess initiatives, products, or projects. As an illustration, a proprietor of a small business may employ the SWOT analysis in order to determine whether or not entering a new market is a prudent choice. They would evaluate their internal strengths, such as the distinctiveness of their products or the strength of their customer base, as well as their shortcomings, which could include a lack of brand awareness in the new market or the limited resources they have available. In addition to this, they would do an analysis of external opportunities, such as an increasing demand for their products in the new market, as well as risks, such as severe competition or economic instability.

Because of this analysis, they are able to make well-informed decisions. These well-informed decisions can help the company develop a strategic plan for entering the new market. The analysis of internal strengths and weaknesses allows the company to capitalise on its strengths and address any weaknesses before entering the market. By identifying areas for improvement, the company can allocate resources to enhance their brand awareness and overcome any limitations they may have. Additionally, the analysis of external opportunities and risks enables the company to identify potential growth areas and potential obstacles that may arise in the new market. This information can be used to formulate strategies to take advantage of the opportunities and mitigate the risks.

When and why should you do a SWOT analysis?

A SWOT analysis is often used at the start of or as part of the process of making a strategic plan. People think that the framework is a strong tool for making decisions because it helps a company find success opportunities that weren't there before. It also brings problems to light before they become too much to handle. With the help of SWOT analysis, a business can find a niche market where it has an edge over its competitors. It can also help people plan a job path that makes the most of their strengths and warn them of threats that could stop them from being successful. For this kind of analysis to work best, it needs to be used to logically identify and include business problems and concerns. Therefore, a diverse, cross-functional team that can easily share their thoughts and ideas usually performs SWOT analysis. The best teams would base their SWOT analysis on real-life experiences and facts, like numbers for revenue or costs.

This investigation is not restricted to businesses alone. It is possible for sales teams to carry out a SWOT analysis in order to have a better understanding of the competitive position that the team holds within their geographical operational area. By evaluating their strengths, weaknesses, opportunities, and threats, sales teams can identify areas for improvement and develop strategies to stay ahead of the competition. Conducting a SWOT analysis can also help sales teams determine the market demand for their products or services, enabling them to align their sales strategies accordingly.

Additionally, understanding the external factors that could impact sales performance, such as changes in consumer behaviour or economic conditions, allows sales teams to proactively adapt their approach and seize new opportunities. For example, a sales team conducting a SWOT analysis may identify that their main competitor has recently launched a new product that is gaining popularity in the market. This insight allows them to develop strategies to differentiate their own product and maintain their competitive edge.

Furthermore, by understanding the external factors affecting their industry, such as a shift towards online purchasing due to changes in consumer behaviour, the sales team can adapt their approach by investing in digital marketing and e-commerce platforms to reach a wider audience and increase sales.

Getting acquainted with the framework, how it ought to be utilised, and the constraints that it imposes is something that I would strongly recommend to every new sales leader.

5. Strategies for Accurate Sales Forecasting

Moving beyond planning, accurate sales forecasting is the compass that helps you navigate through the unpredictable currents of the market. It's a blend of art and science, utilising historical data, technological tools, and strategic thinking. The key to accurate sales forecasting is to have a deep understanding of your target audience and their purchasing behaviours. By analysing historical data and trends, you can identify patterns and make informed predictions about future sales. Additionally, leveraging technological tools such as CRM software can provide real-time data and insights to further enhance your forecasting accuracy. Finally, strategic thinking is crucial in adjusting your sales strategies based on market conditions and competitor analysis, ensuring that your forecasts align with the reality of the market.

While analysing historical data and trends can provide valuable insights, it is important to note that external factors such as economic conditions and unforeseen events can significantly impact purchasing behaviours and make accurate predictions challenging. Therefore, it is essential to constantly monitor and adapt your forecasting models to account for these variables. This can involve regularly updating your data sources and incorporating real-time information into your analysis. Additionally, staying informed about industry trends and customer preferences can help you anticipate potential shifts in demand and adjust your forecasts accordingly. By combining historical data analysis with strategic thinking and a flexible approach, you can improve your forecasting accuracy and make informed decisions for your business.

6. Historical Data Analysis

To begin, you should investigate the historical statistics on sales. It is important to conduct trend analysis, determine peak seasons, and gain an understanding of the elements that drove previous successes or obstacles. The analysis of historical data offers significant insights into the behaviour of customers, which enables you to anticipate future trends and make decisions based on accurate information. By analysing historical data, you can identify patterns and trends that may have influenced sales in the past. This information can help you make more accurate forecasts and develop strategies to capitalise on peak seasons or address any challenges that may arise. Additionally, understanding customer behaviour from historical data can guide you in tailoring your offerings and marketing efforts to better meet their needs and preferences.

Furthermore, analysing historical data can provide insights into the effectiveness of past marketing campaigns and promotional activities. By examining data on customer response rates, conversion rates, and ROI, you can determine which strategies have been successful and which ones need to be adjusted or discontinued. This knowledge can help you allocate your marketing budget more effectively and focus on tactics that are proven to drive results. Additionally, historical data can reveal valuable information about customer demographics, allowing you to target specific segments more accurately and tailor your messaging accordingly.

While historical data can provide insights into past customer behaviour, it may not necessarily predict future trends or account for external factors that can impact marketing strategies. This is why it is important to also consider real-time data and industry trends when developing marketing strategies. By combining historical data with current market insights, businesses can make more informed decisions and adapt their tactics to stay ahead of the competition. It is crucial to continuously monitor and analyse data to ensure that marketing efforts remain relevant and effective in an ever-changing landscape.

One counterargument to the importance of continuously monitoring and analysing data is that it can be time-consuming and resource-intensive for businesses, especially for sales leaders who also have other operational responsibilities. Additionally, relying solely on historical data and industry trends may not account for unexpected events or shifts in consumer behaviour. For example, a sales leader may spend hours each week reviewing data on customer preferences, market trends, and competitor activities to identify potential areas for improvement in their marketing strategy. They may also analyse the effectiveness of different marketing channels and campaigns to determine which ones are generating the highest return on investment. However, despite all this effort, they could miss out on emerging trends or fail to adapt quickly enough to sudden changes in consumer behaviour, leading to missed opportunities and decreased sales.

7. Utilising Technology in Forecasting

Take advantage of the technical resources that are available to you. It is possible to greatly improve the accuracy of your sales projections by utilising Customer Relationship Management (CRM) systems, data analytics tools, and artificial intelligence. The utilisation of these tools not only facilitates the streamlining of data analysis but also makes it possible to monitor sales operations in real time, thereby offering a dynamic and responsive approach to forecasting.

By integrating CRM systems into your forecasting process, you can gather valuable customer data that can inform your sales projections. These systems allow you to track customer interactions, preferences, and purchase history, providing insights into their buying patterns and behaviour. With this information, you can make more informed predictions about future sales trends and adjust your strategies accordingly. Additionally, data analytics tools enable you to analyse large volumes of data quickly and accurately, identifying patterns and correlations that may not be immediately apparent. This can help you uncover hidden opportunities and potential risks, further enhancing the accuracy of your forecasts.

8. Collaboration with Other Departments

Effective sales forecasting goes beyond the confines of the sales department. Collaborate with marketing, finance, and other relevant departments to gain a holistic perspective. Marketing insights can inform sales forecasts, while financial collaboration ensures that forecasts align with broader budgetary considerations. For example, by collaborating with the marketing department, sales can gain insights on upcoming campaigns or promotions that may impact sales forecasts. This allows the sales team to adjust their forecasts accordingly and ensure accurate predictions. Additionally, by working with the finance department, sales can align their forecasts with budgetary constraints and ensure that their projections are realistic and achievable. Here are just some ideas for why you should collaborate with other departments:

1. Collaborating with the marketing department not only helps sales adjust their forecasts but also allows them to proactively plan and strategize for upcoming campaigns or promotions.

2. Sales can leverage insights from the marketing department to identify potential market opportunities, understand customer preferences, and tailor their forecasts accordingly.

3. Working closely with the finance department enables sales to factor in budgetary constraints and prioritise revenue-generating activities that align with overall company goals.

4. Sales can collaborate with the operations department to ensure efficient supply chain management, avoiding stockouts or excess inventory that could impact sales forecasts.

5. By integrating data from customer relationship management (CRM) systems, sales teams can analyse historical sales data and customer behaviour patterns to forecast future demand more accurately and identify cross-selling or upselling opportunities.

9. Scenario Planning

Scenario planning becomes an extremely useful technique in the context of a corporate environment that is always shifting.

Be prepared for a variety of market scenarios and make preparations for unforeseen circumstances. What would happen if there was an unexpected drop in the economy or if a new competitor appeared on the scene? The use of scenario planning enables you to build plans for a variety of potential outcomes, which helps to ensure that your sales staff is flexible and robust. By incorporating scenario planning into your team's strategy, you can proactively identify potential risks and opportunities, allowing your team to adapt quickly and effectively. This strategy not only improves the capability of your sales staff to negotiate uncertain market situations, but it also helps to cultivate a culture that values agility and innovation. In the event that the team has a scenario plan that has been thoroughly created, it will be able to confidently respond to unforeseen obstacles, thereby seizing new possibilities and remaining ahead of the competition. Additionally, scenario planning fosters proactive decision-making, which gives your sales personnel the ability to make educated choices based on the outcomes that are predicted to occur in a variety of alternative situations. The resilience of your organisation is eventually improved by this strategic instrument.

Many companies and their sales teams were caught off guard when COVID-19 appeared on the scene. This is because many companies had not made preparations for the possibility of such an event occurring. As a result, they were left scrambling to adapt their strategies and operations to the new reality. However, companies that had implemented effective planning processes were better equipped to respond quickly and make informed decisions. These organisations were able to pivot their sales strategies, adjust their target markets, and explore new revenue streams to mitigate the impact of the pandemic. Thus, the importance of planning in fostering resilience and proactive decision-making cannot be overstated, as it ensures businesses are prepared for unforeseen challenges and can navigate through them effectively.

10. Continuous monitoring and adjustment

Forecasting sales is not a one-time occurrence; rather, it is a process that occurs continuously. Your sales performance should be continuously monitored against the forecasts, and you should be ready to alter your strategy in reaction to any new information that comes to light. It is essential to possess flexibility and agility in order to successfully traverse the twists and turns that the market presents. As a result of your sales team's adaptability and resilience, you are able to continuously assess and alter your sales strategy. You will be able to rapidly discover any deviations or possibilities for improvement if you continually analyse the performance of sales in comparison to the forecasts. This proactive approach assures that your team will be able to quickly alter their plan in order to capitalise on changes in the market and maintain a competitive edge.

Forecasting on a weekly basis is almost obligatory in environments that are characterised by rapid change. It is a good habit to do the same with your staff, particularly after evaluating the performance of the previous week and having an expectation of what might possibly occur in the marketplaces in which they operate in the following week. Nonetheless, the teams should not allow this practice to divert their attention away from the overarching objectives that have been established for the year. While evaluating performance and anticipating market changes are important, focusing too much on weekly evaluations may prevent teams from keeping their long-term goals in sight. It is crucial for teams to strike a balance between short-term assessments and overarching objectives.

11. Risk Mitigation Strategies

There is no such thing as a perfect forecast, and the business world is full of inherent hazards. To address difficulties that were not anticipated, you should develop robust risk mitigation methods. The creation of buffer inventories, the diversification of your customer base, and the development of contingency plans for unexpected fluctuations in market demand are all examples of what this could entail. These risk mitigation strategies aim to minimise the impact of unforeseen events on your business operations. By maintaining buffer inventories, you can ensure a steady supply of products even during unexpected disruptions in the supply chain. Diversifying your customer base reduces the reliance on a single client or market, spreading the risk across different sectors. Additionally, creating contingency plans allows you to respond swiftly to sudden shifts in market demand, ensuring continuous profitability and stability.

However, danger is not always associated with a single catastrophic event. There are persistent dangers and challenges that sales teams must contend with, which may be a factor in sales failures. Through the implementation of a data-driven strategy in their processes, the majority of these hazards can be avoided or resolved. We have compiled a list of the top five hazards that sales teams face, along with information on how to evaluate, mitigate, and react to these risks.

1. Inadequate sales strategy

Not understanding your market and your customers can result in an ineffective sales strategy is one of the most important risks for sales teams to be aware of. While your company probably wants to know its market and its customers, your research team may not be digging deeply enough into who your customers are, what they want, and the price they'll pay for it. A team that relies on assumptions and guesses is a team at risk.

Moreover, just because you knew your customers a few months or years ago, doesn't mean you understand the playing field now. Frank Cespedes, Harvard Business School professor, says, "The market is doing what the market will do and sales must respond issue by issue and account by account." Strategic planning is an ongoing process that is linked to research and is actionable in the field.

Be sure to consistently check in on your strategic plan and confirm that you're moving in the right direction and still on target. Ensure that your research is current and up-to-date. Prep your sales team with the tools they need to respond to the ever-changing market and customer evolution.

2. Profit and sales metrics

Collecting inaccurate or inadequate information regarding profit margins and/or sales prices pollutes your company's data and affects the sales team's performance. That's because data is the most valuable currency in the new economy. Rich, accurate, easy-to-retrieve information is worth more than gold to a sales team. But much corporate data is inaccurate.

"Poor-quality data is a huge problem," said Bruce Rogers, Chief Insights Officer at Forbes Media. "It leaves many companies trying to navigate the information age in the equivalent of a horse and buggy."☐ In fact, poor data may cost U.S. corporations as much as $3 trillion each year. Bad data regarding profit margins and sales prices skew the team's ability to offer buyers the right product at the right price to net the profit margin the company needs.

3. Sales and marketing alignment

Sales personnel are often unaware of marketing strategies or if they are, they may simply disregard them. Ray Meiring, CEO and Co-Founder of Quorus Software, writes, "We face this problem precisely because we wait until leads get to the bottom of the funnel before marketing and sales interact with each other. As a result, prospects are exposed to a disjointed handover."

When the sales team works hand-in-hand with marketing to create content, they help set customer expectations early on, which can prevent harmful risks for sales teams. Similarly, when marketing introduces lead scoring, it can help sales prioritise their follow-up interactions. Many companies are also turning to account-based marketing, a strategy that aligns marketing and sales to focus on target accounts and then design a personalised campaign around those accounts.

4. Sales underperformance

According to Forbes, 57% of sales professionals miss their annual quotas. Experts attribute much of this underperformance to having too few opportunities in the pipeline. In other words, the risks for sales teams being unaware of potential customers can hinder other opportunities that can drive revenue. Some companies rely so heavily on virtual sales that they limit seasoned sales professionals' opportunities from getting valuable face-to-face time with prospects and customers.

Others depend too heavily on their team members' soft skills without looking at hard data while others may forget to add a warm human touch to their data-based strategy. Both approaches can drive away prospects, reducing the flow of leads coming through the sales funnel. A data-driven but inspirational strategy leverages your team members' strengths and ultimately keeps your sales professionals interacting with a high volume of prospects.

5. Inadequate product knowledge

Nothing kills a sale faster than a salesperson who fumbles when asked to describe the product. Yet, sales staff often lack knowledge about the features and benefits of the product or service they sell. Not able to hold masterful conversations, these sales professionals leave prospective customers confused or ill-informed about their prospective purchase. In some cases, a salesperson may know the product but not be able to see its benefits from the customer's perspective, and that can be just as damaging."

Communication and transparency

Transparent communication is the glue that holds your sales planning and forecasting strategies together. Keep stakeholders informed about the rationale behind your forecasts, potential challenges, and the steps being taken to mitigate risks. This fosters trust and ensures everyone is on the same page, working collaboratively towards common goals.

In conclusion, sales planning and forecasting form the bedrock of successful sales management. By understanding the nuances of your market, setting clear objectives, and implementing robust forecasting strategies, you empower your sales team to navigate challenges and seize opportunities. The dynamic interplay of planning and forecasting is your toolkit for not only surviving but thriving in the ever-evolving world of sales management. As you embark on this journey, remember that adaptability, strategic thinking, and a customer-centric approach are your North Stars, guiding you towards sustained success.

In addition to these key principles, it is crucial to continuously analyse and assess the performance of your sales team. By regularly reviewing sales data and metrics, you can identify areas for improvement and make informed decisions to optimise your team's performance. Furthermore, fostering a culture of collaboration and open communication within your sales organisation can also contribute to long-term success. Encouraging your team members to share their insights, experiences, and challenges can lead to innovative solutions and a stronger, more cohesive team.

Chapter 5: Skill Assessment and Development

Professionals in the field of human resources frequently provide assistance to their organisations by assessing the performance of employees as well as their abilities and comprehension of significant procedures. A study of the skills gap is one of the tools that human resources personnel can use to gain a better understanding of how employees contribute to the organisation. Individuals who are in charge of teams can reap significant benefits from gaining an understanding of how to carry out a skills gap study.

By conducting a skills gap study, leaders can identify areas where their team members may require additional training or development opportunities. This knowledge can help them create targeted learning programmes that address specific skill gaps, ultimately enhancing the overall performance and productivity of their teams. Additionally, understanding the skills gap can also aid in succession planning, as it allows leaders to identify potential future leaders within their organisation who possess the necessary skills and abilities for advancement.

Why is it important to conduct a skills gap analysis?

It is essential to do a skills gap analysis because it enables leaders, in conjunction with human resources and the training departments, to have a better understanding of the talents that the company requires and how the sets of skills that employees now possess relate to those requirements. Among the many reasons to carry out a skills gap study are the following:

To obtain insight into staff expertise:

A skills gap analysis can help you identify which team members have the greatest degree of ability in specific areas and determine which tasks people are most suited for. Knowing the varied skill levels of employees can also assist leadership teams in determining where to focus improvement efforts.

To support learning and development:

Individuals can use the findings of their skills gap analysis to discover the abilities required for their job and develop in their careers. Learning and development teams at companies can focus their efforts on bridging skill gaps by focusing training efforts on areas where employees are not meeting the company's needs.

To improve hiring and recruitment:

Conducting a skills gap analysis during the recruitment process might assist the sales manager in making educated judgements. Skills gap analysis can not only analyse how well-matched individual applicants are for sales roles, but it can also be useful when comparing prospects to make the best recruiting decisions for the organisation.

To serve as a foundation for planning:

A skills gap study can tell the sales manager not only about whether team members' talents fit current business needs, but it can also indicate whether personnel may need training to prepare them for future business developments.

Assessing the Skills Gap

When screening applicants for sales positions, you must determine if they have the necessary skills, traits, and mindset. You can learn much about candidates during the interview by asking the right questions and listening actively to responses. However, your first impression of candidates doesn't always reflect their ability to do the job. A candidate might be friendly and a good communicator, but how do you know if they can sell your product or service? In this section, I will be focusing on the process of screening new applicants for your team. However, the same evaluation may also be applied to an existing team, as it will assist the new sales manager in better understanding the dynamics of the skills that are present within the team.

A sales skills assessment evaluates candidates based on specific talents to see whether they have the potential to be great salespeople. Various organisations have their own sales assessment exams, and it is critical for the newly promoted or appointed sales manager to become acquainted with these tools. While each of these may take a different approach, it is critical for the sales manager to keep an eye out for the following soft and hard abilities:

Customer relationship-building management

Building rapport with clients is an important skill to look for in sales prospects since it relates to customer pleasure, loyalty, and greater sales. A positive relationship fosters trust and creates a favourable impression of your company. Customers who connect with a salesperson are more likely to acquire a product or service. To accomplish this purpose, sales personnel must possess sales abilities such as verbal communication in order to deliver product information and value, engage clients, and persuade them to purchase your goods without being pushy or putting them under pressure. Active listening and empathy are also required to encourage consumers' honesty so that salespeople can understand their needs, address worries, develop tactics to alleviate doubts, and, finally, secure a deal that satisfies both sides.

Driving business growth

Those who work in sales have the objective of generating revenue, which they accomplish by advertising and selling items or services to specific customers. To do this, however, one must possess abilities such as communication in order to guarantee consumer involvement and negotiation in order to successfully close sales. When revenue is generated, it has a direct impact on the bottom line of the company since it increases the possibility of profit. Additionally, driving business growth requires sales professionals to constantly analyse market trends and identify potential opportunities for expansion. They must also build and maintain strong relationships with existing customers to ensure repeat business and referrals. Ultimately, the success of a sales team is crucial for the overall success and profitability of a company.

Building and maintaining the company's brand image

The salespeople of your company are the face of your company since they interact directly with the outside world, which includes both existing customers and potential customers. You need to have members of your team that are able to establish trust and confidence in order to achieve success. This is because it is essential to be able to keep a loyal client base.

People are more inclined to take your goods and services seriously if they have a favourable impression of the company, which can result in higher success for the business. Further, they are more likely to make additional purchases of products or services, to leave positive reviews online, and to generate word-of-mouth recommendations, all of which lead to an increase in the number of customers that patronise your business.

Because of this, it has the ability to attract top talent to your firm; salespeople who are enthusiastic about their work will want to join forces and work with you. This is because they will want to work with you. They will be attracted to the positive reputation and customer loyalty that your business has built. Additionally, working with enthusiastic salespeople can create a positive and motivated work environment, leading to increased productivity and overall success for your firm.

Dealing with objections

Customers do not always want the goods or services on offer; hence, salespeople are frequently rejected. There are numerous obstacles to completing a deal, including:

Lack of need: The customer believes that they do not require the goods or service.

Lack of trust: The customer is distrustful about the product, the salesperson, or the company in general.

Lack of comprehension: The customer does not understand what the salesman is offering.

Price: The customer believes the price is too high or that they cannot afford to purchase it right now.

Consumer procrastination occurs when a consumer is not yet ready to commit to acquiring a product.

Excellent sales skills will equip candidates to handle objections in the most appropriate way. For example, they may use their communication skills to explain the product or service in more detail, convincing the customer of its value. A thorough understanding increases the likelihood of turning a prospect into a paying customer.

Foster a positive culture.

In order to foster a joyful environment at work, one strategy is to make certain that your sales staff is comprised of salespeople who are skilled in their craft. One example is that employees who have more experience have a greater chance of meeting or exceeding their goals. This can boost the motivation of a sales team, which in turn can lead to an overall improvement in performance. Furthermore, it is a well-known fact that salespeople who are enthusiastic about their work have the potential to generate an 18% increase in sales.

The procedure of onboarding applicants who have sales talents is another factor that contributes to the significant competence that the team possesses. The employees have the opportunity to collaborate with one another to solve obstacles, exchange their knowledge with one another, search for inspiration in one another, and discuss the sales methods that have proven to be the most successful for them.

Product Knowledge

Salespeople need to understand the product or service they're selling very well. Whether it's an insurance product, car or a skincare range, your team members should fully understand what it is, how it works, its features, and its competitive advantages. With product knowledge, your salesperson can:

Deliver an engaging sales pitch.

Answer consumer questions.

Deal with objections.

An ideal salesperson will go above and beyond the basics to educate consumers about your product or service.

For example, they might share their experience of using the product themselves, communicate extra details, and compare it to competing brands. If they are selling a cooking appliance, they may offer a presentation of the product in use, which proves how the item has solved their complex cooking needs.

Understanding the market through research

Participating in market research is one methodology that may be utilised to enhance product knowledge. It is necessary for salespeople to conduct extensive market research in order to gain an understanding of the current market circumstances and trends in the industry, as well as to become familiar with the products offered by rivals. By doing so, salespeople gain an advantage because it helps them understand the market, which in turn helps them: Putting your products in a more advantageous position Convince customers by providing them with pertinent information. Decide what it is that customers want. In addition, depending on the direction that the study takes, it may also assist your sales team in locating new customers through whom it might attract and enter specialised markets. Because of these efforts, your company will see an increase in revenue as well as an intensification of its brand recognition.

Data analysis

If salespeople have critical skills, they can do market research more quickly because they'll be able to read data, spot trends, draw conclusions, and change their pitches to fit these conclusions. Analysis of sales data is a useful tool that can have an effect on the work of a whole sales team. It gives team members information they can use to make decisions that will help the general plan get more customers and sales.

Networking

Building your company's reputation relies on good connections with existing customers, potential customers, business partners, investors, and other industry professionals. Salespeople need strong networking skills to maintain professional relationships with these groups, meet new people, and drive new business.

Networking is crucial for sales because it enables companies to connect with potential customers and deliver information.

For example, a small business owner wanting to increase sales may attend industry conferences and trade shows to network with potential customers and showcase their products or services. By engaging in conversations, exchanging contact information, and following up with personalised emails or phone calls, the business owner can establish a rapport with potential customers and ultimately convert them into paying clients. Additionally, networking can also lead to valuable referrals and partnerships that further enhance sales opportunities for the business.

Communication

When it comes to becoming a successful salesperson, communication is the most important factor. This is due to the fact that interaction with customers, whether in person or over the phone, is an essential component of the work. Not only is it necessary for them to articulate the specifics of the items or services they offer, but they must also utilise their words to convince people to purchase them and to answer the problems and requirements of customers.

It is also vital to have abilities in written communication in order to send emails, create presentations, and make reports after gathering data on the market. Make sure that your candidates have a strong command of writing skills, including the ability to spell and use proper language. It is possible that reading our guide on workplace communication exams will prove beneficial to you.

A few other communication skills are required of salespeople, including the ability to listen to others as well as the ability to comprehend information and respond appropriately. Candidates with active listening abilities will be able to comprehend the requirements of the client and find solutions to problems, such as when the customer had previously attempted to use a product that was comparable but did not produce the desired outcomes.

Presentation Skills

Although a salesperson may be skilled at selling things, they may also be able to produce captivating presentations that represent the firm, display products, and make a positive first impression that is favorable. When it comes to sales candidates, it is essential to evaluate their presentation skills because a great presentation has the potential to bring in new clients and customers, impress investors, and communicate essential information about your firm.

Furthermore, strong presentation skills also demonstrate the salesperson's ability to effectively communicate complex ideas in a concise and engaging manner. This is crucial in building trust and credibility with potential clients, as well as effectively conveying the value and benefits of the products or services being offered. Ultimately, a salesperson with exceptional presentation skills is more likely to successfully close deals and contribute to the overall growth and success of the firm.

Creativity

Creativity is essential for sales professionals since it assists in the resolution of issues, the development of plans, the surmounting of challenges, and the enhancement of negotiation strategies. Additionally, it is beneficial to have people on your team who are creative and capable of coming up with ideas in order to keep up with changes in the industry. If you want to better match your plans with digital commerce, for instance, you might need to reassess your strategies. Because 68 percent of company-to-business customers would rather conduct business online than with a salesperson, selling companies need to update their procedures in order to maintain their relevance and ensure the safety of their trade.

Time management

Given that targets are frequently what drive the sales industry, it is crucial to choose candidates who can effectively manage their time, accomplish their objectives, and meet their deadlines. The achievement of monthly, quarterly, or annual sales targets calls for a high level of organisation on the part of the business. Prospecting and completing deals in a timely manner are the two most important duties for salespeople to focus on, and they should prioritise these jobs above all others. Candidates that have good time management abilities are able to better manage their time in high-pressure circumstances, and these talents frequently result in candidates exceeding their expectations. Salespeople who excel at time management are able to effectively allocate their resources and prioritise tasks, ensuring that they meet their sales targets consistently. By efficiently managing their time, they can devote more attention to prospecting and closing deals, ultimately leading to higher sales performance and surpassing their own goals.

Patience

For the sake of meeting sales goals that are getting closer, there is a risk that salespeople who are desperate will put pressure on customers to buy a product. If, on the other hand, customers have the impression that they are being coerced into making a decision in a hurry, they may lose faith in your company and lose interest in making purchases from you.

Consequently, it is of the utmost importance to search for salespeople who possess patience and are able to maintain their professionalism throughout the buyer's decision-making process. It can be challenging to find a happy medium between patience and persistence, but the ideal applicant will demonstrate that they possess a combination of these two characteristics.

Multilingual skills

In the event that your potential sales representative is fluent in one or more languages, they will be able to speak with various markets, connect with a greater number of people, establish a connection with customers, and overcome linguistic resistance. If you operate in a market that is diverse, this is something that you should take advantage of. Having multilingual skills can also help your sales representative understand cultural nuances and adapt their sales approach accordingly. This can lead to stronger relationships with clients and increased sales opportunities in different regions or countries. Additionally, being able to communicate in multiple languages can give your company a competitive edge in the global marketplace.

As the newly promoted sales manager, it is critical that you use the assessment methods already in place at your company to look for these characteristics in both newly appointed personnel and other members of your team. You will be able to construct your development interventions, coaching sessions, and market deployment more successfully if you have a deeper understanding of the skill gaps.

Creating a Training Programme for Your Team

The steps I would recommend for building an efficient sales training programme for your team are outlined below. Having completed the skills evaluation and having the findings will also inform your strategy. While these steps serve as a foundation, you can modify them to meet your specific goals and the availability of resources inside your organisation.

I am convinced that a hybrid strategy, in which your end result has diverse parts of intervention styles and delivery, is far more effective. For example, you could incorporate a mix of in-person workshops, online modules, and mentorship programmes to cater to different learning styles and ensure maximum engagement. Additionally, regularly analysing the performance data of your sales team can help identify specific areas for improvement and tailor the training programme accordingly.

This hybrid approach allows for a more personalised and adaptable training experience, as it recognises that individuals have unique learning preferences and needs. By combining various intervention styles, you create a comprehensive and well-rounded training programme that addresses different skill levels and promotes continuous growth. Moreover, analysing performance data provides valuable insights into the effectiveness of the training initiatives, enabling you to make data-driven decisions and continuously improve the programme to meet the evolving needs of your sales team.

Steps for Designing an Effective Sales Training Programme for Your Team

Sales teams need training that is tailored to their needs and objectives so they can be successful. This article provides steps for designing an effective sales training programme that focuses on the strengths of your team members.

Thereby, providing tools to help them stay motivated and engaged in their work promotes collaboration and trust amongst team members.

By following these tips, you can build an effective sales training programme that will help your team reach their goals and maximise their potential.

What is a sales training programme?

A sales training programmeme is a systematic programmeme that is aimed at assisting sales teams in improving their performance and making the most of their potential. Rather than focusing on the weaknesses of each individual member of the team, it offers tactics and tools that are designed to assist them in remaining motivated and engaged in their job.

Not only does it foster a culture of trust and collaboration among members of the team, but it also contributes to the development of a sales team that is both successful and productive. The training programme should be tailored to each team's needs and objectives, and it should be regularly updated to reflect changes in the market, customer behavior, and the team's goals.

When contemplating sales training, it is essential to have a clear idea of the outcomes you wish to achieve on the sales front. If you want to take any kind of action, you must first answer this one simple question:

What is it that we hope to accomplish?

There is a wide range of potential goals that sales training can focus on, including but not limited to raising the average size of sales, adding accounts, raising revenue, and boosting profits. When selecting sales training efforts, it is important to ensure that they align with the results you want to achieve. Take into consideration the following potential outcomes and the means by which you can accomplish them as you contemplate your own sales training initiatives:

A large percentage of sales training is focused on accomplishing a single ultimate aim, which is either to raise revenue or to enhance profitability. The question is how you intend to expand your sales while also increasing your profits. You can get there in a variety of ways, each of which requires a unique combination of sales skills and a high level of concentration.

Here are the main categories of techniques to increase revenue and enhance results. You must concentrate on distinct sales talents and processes within each bucket. But, before you choose a talent to learn or a sales training programme to engage in, you need to know which of these nine areas you want to improve:

1. Grow existing accounts.

Growing existing customers is frequently one of the quickest and most profitable strategies to increase revenue. Whether they are strategic or key accounts, your clients are unlikely to purchase as much as they could or should from you. Most businesses would benefit greatly from tapping into those accounts.

2. Increase the average size of the sale.

This entails targeting larger accounts, marketing a broader solution range, and offering lower discounts. Many sales teams have a significant talent gap in the needs-discovery phase of the selling process. Conducting a thorough and rigorous needs discovery process is a critical step in developing the correct solution and increasing sales.

3. Increase the win rate on the proposed business.

Winning more of the sales you propose is a key leverage point for increasing revenue. When sellers know what to do to drive and win their most significant sales prospects, not only does revenue grow, but the cost of selling drops since the sales force is more efficient with their time and energy.

4. Win More Business with New Accounts

This involves increasing the number of new leads you generate, adding prospects to your pipeline, and boosting lead quality. If you want to increase sales, your sales force must continuously bring in fresh leads.

5. Speed Up the Sales Cycle

With a shorter sales cycle, you can bring in more business faster and free up your sales personnel to work on other prospects. This increased sales productivity enables you to do more with your current sales staff.

6. Win Sales at Favourable Terms

Your sellers must be able to sell with value, overcome objections, and negotiate the finest deals in order to gain sales with high profit margins and attractive agreement terms. When sellers know how to negotiate, not only are revenue and margins on sales higher, but the win rate increases as sellers lose fewer sales due to last-minute blunders.

7. Improve the hiring success rate and ramp-up time.

The difficulty of employing good salespeople and sales executives is a limiting factor in the growth of many businesses. Increasing your hiring success rate while minimising hiring failures has a significant impact on your success.

When you recruit a salesperson, you want them to go from "new hire" to "really successful" as quickly as possible. It can take up to a year for new staff to reach maximum sales productivity. The revenue growth rewards from shortening this timeframe are enormous.

Leading and Lagging Measures of Success

The seven variables discussed above are the most prevalent lagging markers of success. They will tell you if your sales training and change management strategies were successful. However, these measures are retrospective in nature, indicating only what has occurred rather than what will occur in the future. Leading indicators are those that indicate whether you are on the right or wrong route towards your desired outcome. There are numerous specific leading indicators that can signal progress, ranging from selecting the best change management and sales training initiatives to establishing the right sales enablement system with technologies, tools, and resources and improving the effectiveness of sales management and leadership.

Here are two big-picture leading indicators that almost always lead to better ultimate results:

8. Increase the effectiveness of sales Leadership, Management, and processes.

Sales management effectiveness is typically the deciding factor between current and projected sales success. Sales managers must maximise sales motivation while also holding salespeople accountable and coaching them to peak performance.

Simultaneously, proper rules and processes must be in place to ensure that sellers can (and will) sell with optimum effectiveness and efficiency.

9. Build a Culture of Sales Achievement

You need your sellers to be on top of their game every day. To keep sellers on track and excelling, you must create a culture of inspiration and support. A high-performing sales culture can have a game-changing impact on sales outcomes.

Focus initially on your targeted goals and which KPIs you need to be driving when you create your sales training programme. There is a vast list of sales indicators you can and should track: win rate, number of qualified meetings, number of proposals submitted, average deal size, gross margin, discounts, account growth percentage, ramp-up time, sales cycle time, and so on.

For the best sales training results, design your programme with the desired outcome(s) in mind, and make sure you have measurements in place to track your progress.

After answering the question, "What do you hope to achieve?" You must address the following:

What are the possible sales training challenges?

What are the most challenging aspects of your sales training programme? If you can define them properly, you may be able to mitigate them. You must plan for any potential stumbling blocks that you, your learners, and instructors may face during the sales training process.

Create a solution for each challenge. So, no matter what comes your way, you'll be able to plan and deliver excellent sales training. Trainers, for example, frequently face schedule and logistics challenges. They could be training remote sales teams or working with sales professionals who travel, live, and work in different time zones.

They can design the training to work around this potential roadblock if they identify it.

Determine the most effective method of sales training.

Which sales training approaches are most suitable, which will help trainers be as effective as possible, and which will ensure trainees meet their learning objectives? In an ideal scenario, you would choose the methodology that is best suited to the subject area, trainee needs, and available resources.

Among the most common training methodologies are:

- ILT (instructor-led training) lectures
- Roleplaying and group discussion

When delivering sales training, it may be advantageous to integrate a few different approaches.

This enables you to better accommodate various learning styles and give employees who might not be able to receive training using a single technique the opportunity.

Use modern sales training technology.

Using current sales training technology is one step in building an efficient sales training programme, but how will you leverage technology to put the training approaches you've chosen into action?

For instance, it's possible that instructor-led training in person won't be practical. It is possible that you will need to incorporate a sales training tool in order to empower employees to engage through the use of communication tools such as Zoom.

It is possible that you will also be required to select and deploy a learning management system in order to provide participants in training with assistance in accessing training and monitoring their progress.

Build out sales training content.

To be able to facilitate sales training in any format, you are required to have a curriculum. You have the option of developing your own sales training in-house, employing a professional sales trainer, purchasing sales training software, or going with a hybrid solution, depending on the specific requirements of your sales training programme.

There are instructional design materials accessible to assist you in the event that you choose to develop your own curriculum entirely within your organisation.

Technology may be a real lifesaver in this particular area of the process of developing sales training, which is another facet of the process. Sales training software allows training experts to create training materials that can be distributed in a variety of ways. Professionals in training can produce these materials.

In addition to that, an effective learning management system will incorporate a model for the creation of courses.

Additionally, it acts as a single repository for various learning assets and materials that are associated with the course.

Develop sales training assessments.

It can be tough to create the assessments needed to establish whether your training is helpful. Most sales training courses will ask you to check your understanding at various points.

Among these evaluations and criteria are the following:

- Whether trainees comprehend the supplied material during the sales training procedure
- Evaluating retention once trainees have returned to work following quick testing of overall mastery

If your evaluations aren't yielding the anticipated results, having a plan in place can help.

Improving your sales training programme is critical for maintaining your sales team's motivation, engagement, and success.

Deliver the sales training programme to me.

This is perhaps the most essential phase, because it is at this point that all of the work that you have done in preparation for this point comes into play. For the sales manager to be able to offer these training engagements with confidence and also to provide the programme for constructive interaction with the team or learners, it is also important for the sales manager to be thoroughly prepared for these training engagements. Thorough preparation includes understanding the specific needs and goals of the team or learners, as well as tailoring the training content to address those needs effectively. Additionally, the sales manager should create a supportive and engaging learning environment that encourages active participation and fosters a sense of ownership among the team or learners. This will ultimately contribute to the success of the sales training programme by maximising knowledge retention and skill development.

Chapter 6: Personal Development

In this final chapter, we now turn our focus to the development of the newly appointed sales manager. Personal development is crucial for the growth and success of any individual, especially in a leadership role. The sales manager should actively seek opportunities for self-improvement, such as attending workshops or conferences, reading relevant books, and seeking mentorship from experienced professionals. By continuously investing in their own personal development, the sales manager can enhance their leadership skills and effectively guide their team towards achieving their goals.

If the sales manager adopts a culture of continuous learning, not only for the team but also for themselves, it demonstrates to the team, from a leadership perspective, that development must be the cornerstone for each and every member of the team. Additionally, it encourages individual members of the team to also act as supporters of this concept of continuous development.

Continuous Learning

Academics, mentors, colleagues, and even members of one's own family frequently use the buzzword *"personal development,"* but what does it actually mean in real-world circumstances? A word that refers to actions that are aimed at improving one's talents, potential, employability, and even riches is called "personal development."

You are engaging in personal development whenever you are intentionally working to better yourself. This includes any time you set out to improve yourself. The significance of personal development cannot be overstated since it enables people to develop into the best versions of themselves, thereby equipping them with the abilities and self-assurance that are necessary to successfully navigate virtually any circumstance.

A significant number of elements, including jobs, real-world experiences and interactions, neighbourhoods, and a great deal of other factors, all have a role in determining how adults perceive life. When we talk of "personal development," we are not referring to a particular period of time during maturity; rather, it is a process that involves a lifetime of commitment and awareness in order to keep up with the inevitable ups and downs that life has to offer.

Personal growth, on the other hand, does not solely refer to the enhancement of the areas of our lives that are purely personal. It is also applicable to professional development and the actions that you can take to advance your career and your knowledge in order to become a more well-rounded and productive employee and leader. Depending on the circumstances, this may mean reaching a significant business milestone, obtaining the promotion you've been working for day in and day out, or taking efforts to improve your skill set.

It is absolutely necessary for every sales leader to possess strong management abilities in addition to excellent people management skills. There is a possibility that you do not possess all of the talents necessary to be a successful sales manager; nonetheless, you have shown that you have the ability to lead and develop into a powerful sales leader. Not only is it essential to acknowledge that leadership qualities will set you apart from others, but they will also assist you in driving genuine organisational advancement.

Can leadership skills be learned?

The subject of whether or not leadership qualities can be acquired through self-study is one of the most frequently asked questions in this context. There is no doubt in my mind that they are able to do so. It's possible that some people are born with a natural ability for leadership, but leadership abilities are something that can be cultivated and perfected over time by consistent practise and dedication.

In fact, relying solely on natural talent or experience is not sufficient to achieve the goal of becoming a great sales leader. If you want to reach your maximum potential, you need to make a permanent commitment to learning and growing.

The power of continuous learning for sales leaders

It is essential to recognise the necessity of continuous education and self-improvement in order to be able to perform well in the role of a sales leader. It is possible that techniques that were successful yesterday would not be effective tomorrow due to the fact that the world of sales is constantly changing. Consequently, if you want to continue to stay one step ahead of the competition, you need to continue to learn and enhance your skills. Leadership is a crucial aspect of any successful sales team. But even natural-born leaders need continuous learning and self-improvement to unlock their full potential.

There is an infinite amount of information available on the internet that you can use as a reference for your efforts to improve yourself as a person. In my opinion, reading is the most suitable gift for anyone who is interested in acquiring new knowledge on a consistent basis. While it is true that participating in structured programmes can assist in the development of your profile and open doors for career progress, it is also true that gaining exposure to fresh information through reading will undoubtedly play a significant role in your own personal development in all aspects of life. Reading not only expands your knowledge and understanding of various subjects, but it also enhances critical thinking skills and promotes empathy by exposing you to different perspectives. Additionally, reading allows you to explore different cultures, experiences, and ideas from the comfort of your own home, making it a convenient and enriching way to continuously grow as an individual.

As a means of providing you with assistance on this path of continuous learning, I have provided a list of an assortment of books and resources that can serve as references at the conclusion of the book. There are an infinite number of reference sources available, and I am confident that by making use of the new technology that is at our disposal, you will discover an infinite number of options that you can refer to.

Balancing Work and life

Thinking of strategies to keep your personal and professional lives distinct could help you grasp the importance of a good work-life balance. You can perhaps achieve a good work-life balance if you are happy with the time you spend on both your professional and personal duties. People who are able to maintain this balance are less likely to let their mental health decline, and they are also less affected by the stress they experience on the job. You could find that this helps you achieve your professional and personal goals simultaneously.

Benefits of maintaining a work-life balance

Here are some reasons why achieving a balance between work and life may benefit your health, mindset, and mood:

1. Maintaining mental health

Individuals who attempt to maintain their mental health may find it easier to manage negative emotions, thoughts, or experiences. Being able to process negativity is important because it can affect your ability to make informed decisions with a clear mindset. For some people, processing emotions may improve their chances of discovering which work-life factors contribute to feelings of stress or unhappiness, making them easier to eliminate.

2. Improving physical health

Maintaining your physical health can help ensure you have enough energy to complete professional and personal tasks efficiently. Eating nutritious meals, forming healthy sleep habits, getting regular exercise, and doing activities you enjoy can all help you achieve a good balance. These examples can provide your body with the support and energy to help you focus on work longer and deal with negative emotions and situations more effectively.

Individuals can also achieve better professional and personal balance when they learn strategies to improve their physical and mental health. For example, stress can limit your ability to manage your physical needs, so it's helpful to prioritise your mental as well as physical well-being.

3. Minimising work-related stress

Work-related stress can sometimes occur when employees feel overwhelmed by their workload and responsibilities. Having some control over these factors can help you achieve a satisfactory personal and professional balance. Some choices that you can make in the workplace to minimise stress include delegating tasks when possible and declining to take on more work than you can reasonably handle. You can learn how to manage your workload more effectively by prioritising the most important or time-sensitive tasks.

Another potential method for managing workloads is to consider your current mental state and physical well-being. For example, suppose you're faced with additional work or responsibilities before leaving the office. You can save those extra tasks for the following day so that you can go home, get enough sleep, and come back refreshed in the morning.

4. Being more present in the moment

Being present in the moment means being mindful of what you're doing currently. Mindfulness is one way to achieve professional and personal balance because it helps you focus on the task at hand. For instance, you may choose to focus on your hobbies when not at work and block out work-related distractions, such as e-mails or office messaging platforms. Being able to focus on professional or personal activities can help you more thoroughly enjoy how you're spending your time.

Achieving a balanced lifestyle can positively impact your personal relationships as well. For example, individuals who work long hours might struggle to give their undivided attention to friends and family. This can also apply to your work relationships. Holding conversations with coworkers about their personal affairs can improve your mood and motivate you to complete tasks more effectively.

5. Increasing productivity and engagement at work

A balance between work and personal life can be easier to maintain if you enjoy the work you're performing. When employees experience high levels of job satisfaction, they may feel more committed to their tasks and inspired to submit their best work. Feeling engaged at work can help create a more efficient approach to task and workload management, which gives you the ability to focus on your personal business outside of work.

6. Becoming a well-rounded individual

Most employees have interests and hobbies that they enjoy in their personal lives, but they can lose them if they dedicate more time and energy to work than to personal business. Spending time on interests and hobbies can help you develop a wider range of skills and expand your knowledge.

Prioritising leisure activities outside of work can also provide employees with unique knowledge that they can share with colleagues. It can also make them more attractive to employers who are looking for candidates with soft skills and diverse life experience.

7. Becoming more successful

There's often a misconception that success requires extreme dedication to hard work. This can be important if you're looking to grow within your workplace, but achieving a work-life balance can allow you to focus on success without sacrificing your well-being. A balanced lifestyle can also boost employee productivity and engagement and support creative thinking. These skills can improve your chances of achieving success without having to overwork yourself.

How to achieve a professional and personal balance

Feelings of stress and fatigue can signify that you want to change how you maintain your professional and personal balance. Every individual has different work-life responsibilities, but implementing the steps below may help you improve your lifestyle balance:

1. Set a goal.

An individual can set and work towards both personal and professional goals that increase their happiness and sense of fulfilment. If you want to establish a goal that will assist you in the maintenance of a better work-life balance, you might think about the circumstances or modifications that you need to make in order to accomplish this objective. For instance, if you want to have more time to spend with your friends, you can consider strategies to reduce or prioritise your task in order to ensure that you leave work with sufficient time to spare.

2. Separate from your work while at home.

Distinguishing between time spent at work and time spent outside of work is necessary for achieving a balanced lifestyle. In order to lessen their need to keep track of their job responsibilities after hours, for instance, an employee who is attempting to concentrate on their friends outside of work can choose to turn off the notifications on their phone. In the event that this is not a viable choice, they may want to consider establishing boundaries with their coworkers or clients during particular hours of the day. This will make it simpler for them to concentrate on their personal business.

3. Use your time at work effectively.

You can make it a goal to be as productive as you possibly can when you are working in order to prevent the activities associated with your job from having an impact on your personal life. As a result of the fact that an excessive workload might, in the long term, lead to a reduction in productivity, it is beneficial to only take on the amount of work that you are able to complete without feeling overwhelmed. It is possible that this will be beneficial to the emotional and physical well-being of an individual, since it will enable them to relax after they have completed their professional commitments. Spending more time with your friends may help you feel more present in the moment, particularly if you have a workload that is less overwhelming and easier to handle.

4. Use techniques for stress management.

If your job causes you to experience emotions of tension or worry, you might want to think about using stress-relieving tactics in order to help improve the balance between your personal and professional lives. For instance, many people find that engaging in regular physical activity acts as a stress reliever. In addition to this, it has the potential to enhance your general physical health as well as your levels of productivity and vitality. One way for employees to improve their ability to regulate their emotions and acquire new abilities is to pursue interests outside of the workplace. For instance, if you find it difficult to maintain a balance between your professional and social duties, you might want to think about acquiring hobbies that include and capture the interest of your friends.

Conclusion

Embracing the journey

Seek out opportunities for personal growth and development outside of your professional function in order to fully embrace the adventure that you are on as a new sales leader. Taking up new hobbies, going to seminars or workshops, or even earning additional schooling in fields that are of interest to you are all examples of things that could fall under this category. You will not only improve your capabilities as a sales leader if you continue to learn new things and broaden your skill set, but you will also be able to introduce new ideas and perspectives to your team. It is important to keep in mind that the journey towards success is not only about arriving at the destination but also about the experiences and growth that occur along the way. Because assisting other people in bettering their lives is essentially the fundamental responsibility of any leader, you should welcome it with open arms and take pleasure in the opportunity to achieve this goal.

In the role of a leader, it is not only a responsibility but also a privilege to assist others in developing and achieving success. If you take advantage of the chance to help other people improve their lives, you will not only be contributing to their success, but you will also be improving your own leadership abilities during this process. Not only does this act of mentoring benefit the people that you are leading, but it also helps to cultivate a positive and supportive dynamic within the team atmosphere. It gives you the opportunity to impart your knowledge and skills to others while simultaneously gaining insight from the distinctive viewpoints and concepts of other people. By accepting this role, you will be able to establish a culture of growth and collaboration among your team, which will ultimately result in increased success for everyone.

Throughout the course of my career, I have had the privilege of heading a number of sales and leadership teams, and I can attest to the immense joy that comes from witnessing the success of others. In fact, you want them to perform better than you and even outgrow you. If you see something like this happening, you will know that you have done an excellent job.

I wish you the best of luck and success on your journey. I have high hopes that this book will not only help you on your path to personal development but also, and perhaps more crucially, help you successfully shift from being a salesperson to a leader. I wish you the best.

Resources

Leadership and Management:

"Leaders Eat Last" by Simon Sinek

- explores the concept of putting people first in leadership and creating a culture of trust and collaboration.

"The 5 Levels of Leadership" by John C. Maxwell

- provides insights into different levels of leadership and practical steps to climb the leadership ladder.

"Dare to Lead" by Brené Brown

- focuses on the importance of vulnerability and courage in leadership.

"Drive: The Surprising Truth About What Motivates Us" by Daniel H. Pink

- examines the science behind motivation and how it can be applied in a leadership context.

"Primal Leadership" by Daniel Goleman, Richard E. Boyatzis, and Annie McKee

- discusses the role of emotional intelligence in effective leadership.

Sales Management:

"The Challenger Sale" by Matthew Dixon and Brent Adamson

- Discusses the characteristics of successful salespeople and how to challenge customers to think differently.

"Crucial Conversations: Tools for Talking When Stakes Are High" by Kerry Patterson, Joseph Grenny, Ron McMillan, and Al Switzler

- Offers practical advice on handling crucial conversations effectively, which is crucial in a leadership role.

"Coaching Salespeople into Sales Champions" by Keith Rosen

- Focuses on coaching techniques to bring out the best in your sales team.

"Fanatical Prospecting" by Jeb Blount

- Emphasizes the importance of consistent and proactive prospecting for sustained sales success.

"Predictable Revenue" by Aaron Ross and Marylou Tyler

- Provides strategies for building a scalable and predictable sales pipeline.

Personal Development:

"Mindset: The New Psychology of Success" by Carol S. Dweck

- Explores the concept of a growth mindset and how it can impact personal and professional development.

"Atomic Habits" by James Clear

- Provides practical insights into building good habits and breaking bad ones, which is essential for personal and professional growth.

"The 7 Habits of Highly Effective People" by Stephen R. Covey

- Offers a holistic approach to personal and professional effectiveness.

"Grit: The Power of Passion and Perseverance" by Angela Duckworth

- Discusses the role of grit in achieving long-term goals.

"Deep Work" by Cal Newport

- Explores strategies for cultivating deep, focused work in an age of constant distractions.

Communication and Influence:

"Influence: The Psychology of Persuasion" by Robert B. Cialdini

- Examines the psychology behind why people say "yes" and how to apply these principles in sales and leadership.

"Never Split the Difference" by Chris Voss

- Written by a former FBI negotiator, this book provides negotiation techniques that can be applied in various leadership scenarios.

"Talk Like TED" by Carmine Gallo

- Offers insights into effective public speaking and communication based on TED Talks.

"Crucial Conversations" by Kerry Patterson, Joseph Grenny, Ron McMillan, and Al Switzler

- Focuses on tools for handling high-stakes conversations with tact and skill.

"Made to Stick" by Chip Heath and Dan Heath

- Explores the characteristics of ideas that stick in people's minds and how to make your messages more memorable.

General Business and Strategy:

"Good Strategy Bad Strategy" by Richard Rumelt

- Breaks down the components of effective strategic planning.

"Measure What Matters" by John Doerr

- Introduces the concept of Objectives and Key Results (OKRs) for goal setting and execution.

"Blue Ocean Strategy" by W. Chan Kim and Renée Mauborgne

- Discusses strategies for creating uncontested market space and making competition irrelevant.

"Thinking, Fast and Slow" by Daniel Kahneman

- Explores the two systems of thinking and how cognitive biases can impact decision-making.

"The Lean Startup" by Eric Ries

- introduces the lean startup methodology for developing businesses and products.

Online Learning Platforms:

LinkedIn Learning

- Offers a variety of courses on leadership, management, sales, and personal development.

Harvard Business Review (HBR) Online

- Access to articles, case studies, and online courses on a wide range of business topics.

Coursera

- Provides courses from universities and organisations on topics ranging from leadership to strategic management.

Udemy

- Offers a diverse range of courses on leadership, communication, and sales management.

Skillshare

- Features short, focused classes on various business and personal development topics.

Bibliography

113 Effective Sales Coaching Tips That Work. n.d. . *Sendoso*. https://sendoso.com/blog/sales-coaching-tips/

ASHER | Sales Training | Aptitude Assessments | Sales Consulting. 2023. . *Asher Strategies Sales Training Blog*. https://www.asherstrategies.com/

Balancing the tension between authority and approachability. n.d. . *Balancing the tension between authority and approachability*. https://www.linkedin.com/pulse/balancing-tension-between-authority-approachability-sekhampu-phd

bretscher michelle. 2021. Effective Communication Strategies for Sales Leaders|Blog. *Amy Franko*. https://amyfranko.com/communication-strategies-for-sales-leaders/

Calvert D. 2019. Promoted! What Is Strategic Sales Management? *Promoted! What Is Strategic Sales Management?* https://blog.peoplefirstps.com/connect2lead/promoted-what-is-strategic-sales-management

Davis KF. 2019. 3 Mindset Changes New Sales Managers Must Make. *TopLine Leadership*. https://toplineleadership.com/3-mindset-changes-new-sales-managers-must-make/

Doerr J. 2018. Want the Best Sales Training? Focus on These 9 Outcomes. *RAIN Group Sales Training*. https://www.rainsalestraining.com/blog/want-the-best-sales-training-focus-on-these-9-outcomes

How to evaluate skills from a sales assessment and test - TG. n.d. . *How to evaluate skills from a sales assessment and test*

- *TG*. https://www.testgorilla.com/blog/evaluate-skills-sales-assessment-test/

Miley J. 2021. Four Key Elements For Evaluating Sales Performance. *Crossroads Coaching.* https://crossroadcoach.com/evaluating-sales-performance/

O'Halloran T. 2021. 7 Sales Coaching Techniques That Elevate Trust And Sales Performance. *Integrity Solutions.* https://www.integritysolutions.com/blog/sales-coaching-techniques/

Olmstead L. 2022. Sales Leadership: 8 Skills to You Need to Lead Sales Teams (2024) - Whatfix. *The Whatfix Blog | Drive Digital Adoption.* https://whatfix.com/blog/sales-leadership/

Root Cause Analysis Template: Uncover Solutions [2023] • Asana. n.d. . *Asana.* https://asana.com/resources/team-communication

Shekhar S. 2022. 7 Simple Steps To Setting Sales Goals This Year (+ Examples). *SalesBlink Blog.* https://salesblink.io/blog/setting-sales-goals

Top 5 Risks For Sales Teams To Be Aware Of | Resolver. 2019. . *Top 5 Risks For Sales Teams To Be Aware Of | Resolver.* https://www.resolver.com/blog/top-5-risks-sales-teams/

Unlock Your Sales Leadership Potential: The Power of Continuous Learning. n.d. . *Unlock Your Sales Leadership Potential: The Power of Continuous Learning.* https://www.linkedin.com/pulse/unlock-your-sales-leadership-potential-power-learning-josh-hirsch

What Is a SWOT Analysis? Definition, Examples and How To | TechTarget. 2023. . *CIO.* https://www.techtarget.com/searchcio/definition/SWOT-analysis-strengths-weaknesses-opportunities-and-threats-analysis

What Is Personal Development and Why Is It Important? 2022. . *What Is Personal Development and Why Is It Important?* https://www.allegromediadesign.com/blog/what-is-personal-development-and-why-is-it-important

A Winning Mindset: Motivating Sales Teams To Reach Goals - Freedom to Ascend. 2023. . *Freedom To Ascend.* https://www.freedomtoascend.com/sales/sales-psychology/motivation/motivating-sales-teams/

www.ingramcontent.com/pod-product-compliance
Lightning Source LLC
Chambersburg PA
CBHW060041210326
41520CB00009B/1219